Amazon Besieged

Praise for this book

'Based on years of first-hand research and vivid testimonies gathered from grassroots communities in Brazil, Sue Branford and Mauricio Torres give a fresh and lucid overview of the complex issues behind mega-development projects and illegal resource extraction that are rapidly destroying the Amazon rainforest and its inhabitants. They expose political corruption and greed, and make a compelling and cogent call for action before it's too late. This is essential reading for those concerned not just for the future of the Amazon and its rich human and ecological diversity, but ultimately for our planet.'

Fiona Watson, Head of Research, Survival International

'*Amazon Besieged* is a compelling book that appeals equally to the head, the heart and to our sense of socio-environmental responsibility. It is a gripping exploration of the dramatic and challenging consequences of the ongoing absorption of the Amazon into market globalisation. In its pages we find the perverse and violent advance of Western modernity through a political nexus that privileges the interests of conservative politicians, construction companies, agribusiness farmers and corporations, at the expense of the rights and livelihoods of indigenous peoples, family farmers, subaltern groups and wider Brazilian society. Written with great wisdom and skills, the text reveals Torres and Branford's lifetime commitment to the production of outstanding work. The book brings together excellent journalism and inquisitive academic research and is a great contribution to understand the planetary repercussions of Amazonian dilemmas. It is an absorbing, page-turner narrative that injects a real sense of indignation and that is a genuine invitation to critical thinking.'

Antonio A R Ioris, School of Geography and Planning, Cardiff University

'*Amazon Besieged* tells a frontier story, a tale of successive waves of land grabbing, cattle ranching, commercial soy farming, and transport and energy infrastructure development, which have degraded the lands, livelihoods and traditional cultures of indigenous people, peasant farmers and fishing communities. While this may sound like a lawless frontier, as Torres and Branford make clear, the Brazilian State is very much present and actively intervenes in support of the agribusiness interests that finance soy's destructive incursion into the rainforest. Based on their reporting of visits to the region in 2016 and 17, Torres and Branford's new book offers a vivid and lively exploration of the dynamics of life and death on Brazil's Amazonian frontier and the threat that this poses to the world's hopes of preventing catastrophic climate change.'

Graham Woodgate, UCL Institute of the Americas

'This is a fascinating, important and astonishing account of the battle to save the living world and the future prospects of humanity.'

George Monbiot, journalist, activist, and campaigner

'This is investigative journalism at its very best! Torres and Branford deliver a meticulously researched yet hugely readable account of their travels through what I would characterise as the "colonial present" of theTapajos region of Brazilian Amazonia. The stakes here could not be higher - if the processes of dispossession and destruction analysed herein are not halted, the region's peoples and forests are doomed. Yet the authors also find hope in forest peoples' vigorous resistance. A must read for all interested in the future of Amazonia.'

Dr James Fraser, Lancaster University

Amazon Besieged

By dams, soya, agribusiness and land grabbing

Maurício Torres and Sue Branford

Practical Action Publishing Ltd
27a Albert Street, Rugby, Warwickshire, CV21 2SG, UK
www.practicalactionpublishing.org

ISBN 978-1-90901-404-6 Paperback
ISBN 978-1-90901-409-1 Library Ebook
ISBN 978-1-90901-413-8 Ebook

Torres, Maurício and Branford, Sue (2018) *Amazon Besieged: By dams, soya, agribusiness and land grabbing*, Rugby, UK: Practical Action Publishing <http://dx.doi.org/10.3362/9781909014091>.

Since 1974, Practical Action Publishing has published and disseminated books and information in support of international development work throughout the world. Practical Action Publishing is a trading name of Practical Action Publishing Ltd (Company Reg. No. 1159018), the wholly owned publishing company of Practical Action. Practical Action Publishing trades only in support of its parent charity objectives and any profits are covenanted back to Practical Action (Charity Reg. No. 247257, Group VAT Registration No. 880 9924 76).

Picture editing and front cover photograph © by Mauricio Torres
Cover design by RCO.design
Printed in the United Kingdom
Typeset by vPrompt eServices Pvt. Ltd., India

Contents

Foreword: "A Storm is Blowing out of Paradise"

Just before he committed suicide as he fled into Spain from Nazi Germany, Walter Benjamin, the Frankfurt school cultural critic, wrote a meditation on the small painting, "Angelus Novus" by Paul Klee, one of the few possessions he carried with him as he crossed the Pyrenees to keep his appointment with his death. The quote from Benjamin which is undoubtedly one of his most famous, says this:

> A Klee painting named 'Angelus Novus' shows an angel looking as though he is about to move away from something he is fixedly contemplating. His eyes are staring, his mouth is open, his wings are spread. This is how one pictures the angel of history. His face is turned toward the past. Where we perceive a chain of events, he sees one single catastrophe which keeps piling wreckage upon wreckage and hurls it in front of his feet. The angel would like to stay, awaken the dead, and make whole what has been smashed. But a storm is blowing from Paradise; it has got caught in his wings with such violence that the angel can no longer close them. This storm irresistibly propels him into the future to which his back is turned, while the pile of debris before him grows skyward. This storm is what we call progress.

It is the "Storm from Paradise" – which actually more aptly here should be called the Storm *in* Paradise – that is the topic of this excellent volume by activist journalists Mauricio Torres and Sue Branford. It does have to be said, however, in this world now of massive fires, epic droughts and colossal flooding in Amazonia and outside it, the pivotal role of Amazonian ecosystems themselves in global climate and hydrologies leads us to worry a good deal more about the weather that is driven in part by the extensive changes in land uses within Amazonia itself that helped feed the storms from Paradise that now increasingly frame the parameters of climate change. This book addresses the underlying processes of that transformation.

For a while, after the end of the authoritarian period, it seemed as if the Amazon narrative would be one of environmental and social institution building, with the emergence of a kind of insurgent citizenship that was far more inclusive than the one imposed during the dictatorship and one that in fact radically reduced deforestation in the 2004-20014 period.

This remarkable decline, at a time when regional populations were increasing and the Amazon GDP was going up, largely due to the strong returns on soy, clandestine timber and gold, seemed to reflect the enactment of new kinds of laws and institutions, a shift from lawless impunity to new forms of environmental probity enhanced by up-to-the-minute GIS (Geographic Information System) technologies. New land institutions and the demarcation of over 200 indigenous reserves, the consolidation of extractive reserves and sustainable development reserves ratifying land rights that inhered in the new 1988 Constitution, formed part of this decline, as did the establishment of national parks and forests and inhabited forests more generally. Here traditional livelihoods and new modern global commodities like the super food açaí, artisanal chocolate and creamy Amazon cosmetic oils could capture top prices and valorize forests and those who made their living from them with their knowledge and practices.

This socioenvironmental future seemed within grasp, but it is important to understand that even then there was still quite a bit of clearing going on (millions of hectares, as it happened), and that the development track that much of the political elite had in mind was focused on modernization schemes that reflected the deepest dreams of the military period: a "tropical" mimic of Germany's industrial Ruhr or a 21st century Tennessee Valley Authority. Amazon development on its southern tributaries would rival the industrial corridors of the developed world. Mining extraction, improved waterways (hidrovias is the Brazilian term for them), dams to choke the world's mightiest rivers into docile electric power sources and the sinews of new highways would integrate Amazonia into southern Brazil as a single economic unity. Mining, cattle, timber and agroindustry – the economic quartet of Brazil since colonial times – would take dominating positions in the global economy, moving Brazil from the perennial "country of tomorrow" to the geopolitical and economic powerhouse of a "today".

While the plans for this Amazon sat in dusty archive rooms in Brasilia during the "socioenvironmental" time, they also sat in the files of Brazil's glossiest capitalist class, awaiting the right political and social moment to move forward. In reality, these plans, with their midwives and their profiteers, never really went away, because the globalized demand for the primary commodities of Brazil was expanding in Asia, especially in China, which had, in the post-cold war universe, become Brazil's largest trading partner. The supply chains for modernizing Asia spread everywhere. As Asian manufactures undermined Brazil's industrial economy, the new form of modernism was reflected less in factories and industrial products than in the millions of acres of GMO soybean that relentlessly began to transform Brazil's ecologically complex woodlands into neo-nature monocrops of soy and pasture. While Amazonian clearing did, in fact, decline, the dynamic was rather like "whack a mole" – control in one place produced "leakage". Constraint and regulation in one place meant that speculators and producers simply moved their operations elsewhere: in Brazil to its Cerrado and Caatinga woodlands, in Bolivia and Argentina to the Chaco, and in Uruguay and Paraguay to the remnant of their Atlantic forests. Complex woodlands, with their carbon, their plants, their animals and their biotic and social histories, were reduced to the epitome of simplicity: a single industrial crop.

There were other forces at play, of course, and this book, with its central focus on the development of the Tapajos River, traditional home of the Munduruku Indians among many other tribes, a place of a long history of gold mining, noble fisheries and scientific exploration. reveals how each sector, and each set of players, ignored laws and rights to set up a particularly virulent, and basically unstable, form of capital accumulation. This is based on land theft, asset theft and corruption as Torres and Branford document in painstaking detail.

In their telling, "History begins in ashes" and the myth of Amazon emptiness as the first speculators and colonizers with their land grants from the state and terrains stolen from the natives begin the transformation rooted in the basic idea that clearing is claiming, and everything else follows from that. Cleared land is a commodity; forest is just forest. The book goes through the deep dynamics of speculation and resource plunder into the explosive development of the agroindustrial /mining frontier, the pharaonic dam projects and the resisters to this agenda in which they have no future, not really.

The book takes a sectoral approach and goes through the how and the what, and names the names, some well-known to many, others new protagonists. While the joke in Brazil is always "for my friends, everything, for my enemies, the law", it is clear what practices these forms of corruption produce and how massively destructive they have become. The inventive use of government decrees, a general posture of impunity and the hijacking of policy development to those who stand most to privately benefit from it are perhaps not entirely new in Brazil, but the erosion of legality is always a problem in societies these days, and especially in frontiers where the "law of the 44" (the Winchester) was until quite recently the norm and is still alive and well today, as eco-martyrs Chico Mendes and Dorothy Stang (and literally hundreds of others) can attest. While the powerful get away with murder, small-holders confront bureaucratic blockages, foot dragging, procedural delays and an unending harassment of violence in their attempts to comply with the law, and are rigorously punished if they fail.

Deforestation has shot up lately, and in many cases natives and traditional people, and peasantries, have lost their allies: World Wildlife Fund, Conservation International, Environmental Defense Fund, now side with soy oligarchs on the fatuous Soy Moratorium, enchanted by the idea that the lion will lie down with the lamb, and that a massively deforesting land use, is somehow sparing land for conservation. Other organizations have stood by their principles, but the forest defenders get a lot less press and support than they should. This book in its meticulous detailing explains why the Angel of History, at least in Amazonia, sees only rubble.

Susanna B Hecht, Professor, Luskin School of Public Affairs,
Institute of the Environment, University of California,
Los Angeles and Professor, International History,
Graduate Institute for International Development Studies, Geneva

Acknowledgements

This is a book based on a series of journalist reports all but one of which were first published by the US environmental agency, Mongabay, and edited by Glenn Scherer, who greatly enriched the text. This book wouldn't exist without Mongabay and Glenn.

An early version of the article on the community of Montanha-Mangabal originally appeared in the December 2017 edition of EcoAméricas, a monthly report on Latin American environmental issues and trends. We thank them for agreeing to its inclusion in the book.

We had the good fortune to meet committed researchers who gave us indispensable assistance. In particular, we would like to thank Juan Doblas, Márcio Santilli and Adriana Ramos from the Instituto Socioambiental (ISA); Cândido Neto da Cunha, from the government's land reform institute, INCRA; Philip Fearnside from the National Institute of Amazonia Research (INPA); Bruna Rocha, an archaeologist at the Federal University of the West of Pará (UFOBA); Antonio Ioris from the University of Cardiff); Daniela Alarcon, a researcher at the National Museum in Rio de Janeiro; Rinaldo Arruda, an anthropologist and the president of Operação Amazônia Nativa (Opan); Brent Millikan (International Rivers - Brasil), Solange Arrolho (fish expert and lecturer at the Federal University of Mato Grosso (UFMG); Francisco Arruda Machado (or Chico Peixe) an environmental adviser at the Public Federal Ministry of Mato Grosso) and Andreia Fanzeris (Opan), among many others. A special thanks goes to Fernanda Moreria, who helped us write the chapter on Montanha-Mangabal.

In our trip along the Teles Pires river, we received crucial logistic support from International Rivers - Brasil and from the Instituto Centro de Vida (ICV), for which we would like to thank Brent Millikan (IR) and João Andrade and Thiarles Santos (ICV).

The articles were published in Portuguese on the website of *The Intercept Brasil*, after being carefully and competently edited by Rebeca Leher and Andrew Fishman. Their editing helped enrich the final texts published here.

We were fortunate enough to be accompanied on our trip by the journalist Thaís Borges, who, as well as making videos and taking photos, played an active role in the interviews. Her contribution is present throughout the book.

We would like to thank our publisher, Practical Action Publishing, for its support and patience in the editing and production of the book.

We also want to express our profound thanks to the families on the Gleba Mercedes agrarian settlement near the town of Sinop, the Munduruku Indians, the families at Montanha-Mangabal, and everyone else who welcomed us into their homes, villages, communities and temporary shacks in the land occupations. Our wish to tell their story, so often muffled by agribusiness's much louder narrative, was one of the main reasons why we made the trip and are publishing this book.

Maurício Torres and Sue Branford

Introduction

The Tapajós river valley is under fierce attack from powerful economic interests which promote agribusiness, mining, and hydroelectric dams. They are felling forest to create pasture for cattle, seeking to turn the valley into an export corridor for commodities, mainly soya, and building hydroelectric dams to provide energy, mainly for mining companies. The construction of new infrastructure – roads, ports, and dams – is proceeding apace, without proper consultation with local communities, many of whom are suffering greatly. Some are resisting, developing new forms of direct action. As little of this is reported in the Brazilian or international press, the authors travelled to the region in 2016 and 2017 to write a series of articles for the US environmental agency, Mongabay.

The Tapajós basin under siege

The Tapajós river basin is in the eye of the storm, as powerful economic interests, backed by the authorities, press ahead with their takeover of the Amazon region. The basin has suffered successive waves of incursion for over 500 years, but today's onslaught is of a different order. Earlier colonial invaders plundered the region, be it for rubber, pelts, or gold, but left most of the forest untouched. In contrast, today's assailants operate what is, in practice, a scorched earth policy. They began to move into the region in the 1970s and have gained greater force in recent years with the growing importance of commodities in the economy. Whenever they can, they evict the traditional populations and lay waste the forest, leaving desolation in their wake.

With the big international mining interests waiting in the wings for changes in the country's legislation, the invaders are seeking to clear forest for cattle ranching and to transform the region into an export corridor for Brazil's huge harvests, cultivated in the country's heartland state of Mato Grosso. Equipped with highly sophisticated machinery, construction companies are building highways, establishing port complexes, and constructing hydroelectric power stations. All at breakneck speed. Along with them comes a motley collection of people – loggers, who generally arrive first to plunder the forest of its most valuable timber, some landless families in search

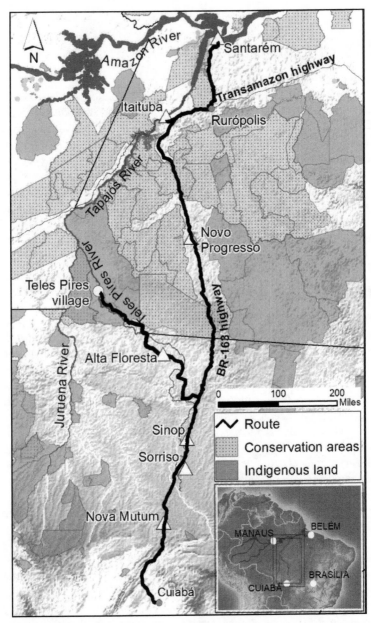

Map 0.1 The Tapajós river basin, and the authors' journey from Cuiabá to Santarém. Map by Maurício Torres

of a plot of land, small-scale miners, and land grabbers, ready to seize their chances. Not far behind come the ranchers, who purchase cleared forest from the land grabbers at highly inflated prices, and agribusiness, which creates soya plantations whenever the terrain permits. Although the soya farmers are Brazilian, they are in hock to multinational companies – Monsanto, which provides technological packages of GM soya, fertilisers, and pesticides, and the international trading companies, particularly Cargill, Bunge, and ADM, which buy and export the soya and maize. It is these companies that make most profit, all with the blessing of the Brazilian authorities.

If the invasion of the Tapajós river valley by powerful economic interests is successful, much of the forest will be felled and many of the region's traditional inhabitants – indigenous tribes, still occupying vast territories, and thousands of fishing families, rubber tappers, and peasant families, all of whom depend on the rivers and the forest for their livelihoods – will be dispossessed. These people, the forest's true guardians, have a profound knowledge of the Amazon ecosystem and know how to use the forest's resources sustainably. If they are driven from the land, memory of them may well be obliterated in a few decades, just as happened in the south of the region, which today belongs to modern Brazil. Along with their annihilation, forest knowledge will be lost.

Most Brazilians, absorbed by the country's prolonged political crisis and struggling to earn a living, know little about what is happening in a region that lies more than 3,000 kilometres (1,800 miles) to the north of São Paulo. And those who do follow events disagree fiercely over the takeover of the region by powerful economic interests. Successive governments have promoted the incorporation of the region into the dominant economic model, arguing that, with millions of Brazilians living in great poverty, the country needs to exploit the Amazon's wealth of natural resources. The two presidents from the Workers' Party (PT, Partido dos Trabalhadores) in power from 2003 to 2016 – Luiz Inácio Lula da Silva and his successor, Dilma Rousseff – broadly continued this policy (though Lula, before he was elected, promised he would be different). Michel Temer, who became president after Dilma was impeached in August 2016, has intensified it, tolerating much greater destructiveness and lawlessness.

The dispute over agribusiness has been particularly fierce. Its advocates say that it is the economy's new powerhouse, bringing in billions of dollars from exports, without which the economy would struggle and perhaps collapse. However, some economists argue that it amounts to carrying on uncritically with the role the country was allocated during colonial rule: to export commodities such as brazilwood, sugar cane, coffee, iron ore, and soya. Just as in the past, Brazil is allowing other countries to carry out the much more profitable business of adding value to these goods. One economist recently drew attention to the absurdity of Brazil spending US$47.5 m (in the first 11 months of 2017) on importing instant coffee from Switzerland, a country that certainly does not produce a bean of coffee (Texeira, 2018). Instead of importing it, he said, Brazil should be exporting instant coffee in large quantities, just as it should be processing soya into meal to feed to pigs, chickens, and cattle, and exporting meat. This would enable Brazil to stop felling forest for more soya cultivation while receiving as much (or more) in export earnings. Agronomists also warn that soya monoculture, with its heavy use of chemical fertilisers and pesticides, is highly dependent on hydrocarbons, which are exacerbating climate change and will one day become depleted. Brazil is mortgaging its long-term future for derisory, short-term profit, they say.

However, the most trenchant criticisms of agribusiness come from environmentalists, social scientists, climatologists, NGOs, and social movements – all concerned about the huge ecological and social cost of what is happening. The Tapajós river basin, which covers almost 6 per cent of Brazilian territory, is widely regarded by biologists as the jewel of the Amazon because of its extraordinary biodiversity (Trandem, 2012). It is also home to dozens of indigenous groups, including the 13,000-strong Munduruku, and to thousands of small peasant and riverine communities. The critics say it is monstrous that, quickly but stealthily and without proper debate, much of this is being destroyed.

What is happening in the Tapajós endangers the world. Many scientists fear that the Amazon forest is near the tipping point, at which so much of the forest is destroyed that it starts to die and to become savannah. Although scientists disagree over precisely when this tipping point will occur, there are already signs that the Amazon forest has stopped being an important carbon sink, absorbing more greenhouse gases than it discharges, and has become a net emitter of greenhouse gases. A few years ago scientists discovered that the earth's forests have played a key role in absorbing greenhouse gases from the atmosphere, acting like a giant sponge and soaking up, on average, about 8.8 billion tons of carbon dioxide each year. A study led by the US Forest Service showed that forests absorbed about a third of fossil fuel emissions annually during the 1990–2007 study period (Clayton, 2011). It is believed that the Amazon forest alone was responsible for about a quarter of that total – absorbing about 6 per cent of global emissions (Kintisch, 2015). Now that the Amazon is losing this capacity, it will make it much harder for the world to reach the goal, agreed in Paris in 2015, to keep the increase in global temperature to below 2°C. More than ever, it is nonsense to go on cutting down forests, yet in the Amazon – as in other tropical countries – it will take a huge effort to halt the advance of the powerful economic interests. One of the problems is the way that one apparently discrete development leads to another: a hydroelectric dam requires infrastructure, particularly roads; this makes agribusiness viable, which leads to more infrastructure; this makes mining viable, which leads to more infrastructure; and so on.

The struggle over the Tapajós may be the crucial battle. The frontier has reached this valley in its march north. It is here that the invaders are attempting to use the facilities created by the federal government for grabbing the land, for reducing the size of protected areas, and for taking over agrarian reform settlements. It is not by chance that this region has recorded the country's highest rates of deforestation in recent years. And the outcome may well be decisive for other regions. If the invaders take over the Tapajós river valley, they will then move on to the valley of the Madeira, another large Amazon tributary, which lies to the west and is already under initial attack, as well as to the Trombetas river to the north, where the main threat at present is not agribusiness but hydroelectric dams and mining. The vicious cycle of never-ending destruction will go on and on.

But very little of what is happening in the remoter reaches of the Tapajós river valley is reported in the Brazilian or international press. Drawing on our experience of working and reporting from the Amazon for many years and with financial backing from the US environmental news agency Mongabay, we made research trips in 2016 and 2017. We wanted to see for ourselves what was going on and to talk to all the main players – the indigenous groups, the riverine communities, the peasant families, the land grabbers, the cattle ranchers, and the soya farmers.

We wanted to witness the process of occupation. We had heard about – and one of the authors had previously studied – the way in which forest is bulldozed by land grabbers, who know that this is by far the best way of illegally acquiring land rights on public land. Without planting a single crop, the land grabbers then sell this cleared land, at a vast profit, to cattle ranchers. Later, if the terrain is suitable, soya farmers purchase the land, establishing their vast monocultures where farming can be readily mechanised. Very few journalistic reports or academic studies have been done on this process, which is crucial to understanding the dynamic of forest destruction. The logic is inexorable: while deforested land is worth very much more – up to 200 times more – than standing forest, it will be impossible to stop profiteers from felling the forest.

We wanted to see the vast soya fields that are marching into the Amazon basin from the south. One of the authors had travelled into the region from Cuiabá along a rough dirt track back in 1979. That trip through dense forest had taken four days in a military lorry, with occasional stops to dig themselves out of deep ruts. She wanted to see for herself the remarkable transformation that the region had undergone during her lifetime. Now we wanted to check out for ourselves the so-called Amazon Soy Moratorium. It has been lauded by powerful actors, from McDonalds to Cargill to Greenpeace, and other countries are thinking of negotiating something similar to stem devastation caused by other export commodities. But we had heard that soya farmers are finding ways of getting around it, that they are not changing their behaviour, that it is essentially greenwash. If these reports are true, then a radical new strategy will be needed to save the forest in the Amazon – and probably to save the world's other forested areas as well.

We wanted to speak to indigenous groups. We knew that the region had once been inhabited only by Indians – indeed, that the very word Tapajós refers to an indigenous group, believed to have become extinct in the 17th century. But for hundreds of years the Indians had been pushed back, confined to smaller and smaller areas by successive waves of migration, and now, it seemed, their way of life was being destroyed by large infrastructure projects, implemented at great haste and without proper consultation with local communities, even though Brazil is a signatory to the International Labour Organisation's Convention 169, which commits the country to holding such consultations before major infrastructure projects are carried out. We'd heard that some Munduruku Indians are in despair, fearful that they were doomed to extinction because of the vicious destruction by a construction company of their most sacred site, where they and their ancestors go after death. Yet they were not even given time to relocate the site elsewhere. We wanted to spend time in their remote indigenous village, located beside a very large, recently constructed hydroelectric dam on the Teles Pires river, and see for ourselves what was happening to them.

We wanted to visit riverine communities, which are also being badly affected by big infrastructure projects, land grabbers, and loggers. We knew that in some areas resistance to the incomers is strong. We had heard that, abandoned by the authorities, some riverine communities are resorting to direct action, at times working with their historic enemies, the Indians, to demarcate their land and expel intruders. We knew that indigenous and riverine communities have achieved some real victories, such as the halting of the plan to build the huge São Luiz do Tapajós hydroelectric dam, and the decision by the authorities to build no more mega-dams in the Amazon. The authorities cited the scale of local opposition to these dams, particularly among the Indians, as one of the factors responsible for this decision. It was time the outside world heard these voices, which are a source of hope in a bleak world.

This book brings together the articles we wrote at the time and have since edited and updated. We began the trip in October 2016, travelling from Cuiabá, the capital of Mato Grosso, to the town of Juara on the Juruena river, one of the two legs of the Tapajós river. We had heard at the last minute that people from traditional communities from all over the Tapajós river basin would be meeting for a festival. It was an excellent opportunity to meet many of the people whose stories we wanted to tell. So we rushed there, the first stop on our journey.

References

All web references were checked and still available in June/July 2018 unless otherwise stated.

Clayton, M. (2011) 'Study: Forests absorb much more greenhouse gas than previously known', *The Christian Science Monitor* [online] <https://www.csmonitor.com/Environment/2011/0715/Study-Forests-absorb-much-more-greenhouse-gas-than-previously-known>

Fraser, B. (2016) 'Q&A: Amazon tipping point may be closer than we think, Thomas Lovejoy says', *Science* [online] <http://www.sciencemag.

org/news/2016/08/qa-amazon-tipping-point-may-be-closer-we-think-thomas-lovejoy-says>

Kintisch, E. (2015) 'Amazon rainforest ability to soak up carbon dioxide is falling', *Science* [website] <http://www.sciencemag.org/news/2015/03/amazon-rainforest-ability-soak-carbon-dioxide-falling>

Teixeira, G. (2018) 'Agro: os números de um mega-retrocesso', *Outras Mídias* [online] <https://outraspalavras.net/outrasmidias/capa-outras-midias/agro-numeros-de-um-mega-retrocesso/>

Trandem, A. (2012) 'Our Rivers Feed Millions', *International Rivers* [webiste] <https://www.internationalrivers.org/resources/our-rivers-feed-millions-7498>

CHAPTER 1
The invisible people gather

The excluded voices – representatives from indigenous, riverine, and peasant communities throughout the Tapajós river basin – meet for a festival in the town of Juara on the Juruena river, and their testimonies illustrate the onslaught they are facing from loggers, land grabbers, and agribusiness.

The Third Juruena Vivo Festival, which took place in the town of Juara on the Juruena river in late October 2016, provided a forum for voices of protest generally absent in Brasília's debate about policies for the region. About 300 participants gathered there, including representatives of the indigenous Apiaká, Kayabi, Munduruku, Manoki, Myky, Nambikwara, and Rikbaktsa peoples; spokespeople from traditional river communities and peasant settlements; researchers; and environmental NGOs.

Ironically, the Juara meeting, launched in rebellion against the takeover of the Tapajós basin by agribusiness and mining – which the Indians see as just another callous act of colonialism – was occurring in the central square of Juara, beside the Statue of The Coloniser. Erected in 2010, the inscription on this big monument reads: 'Our history began here because it was at this very spot that Zé Paraná and other members of the Real Estate Society of the Amazon Basin (SIBAL, Sociedade Imobiliária da Bacia Amazônica Ltda) began their trek into the forest in the midst of the cinders of the first forest felling'. Andrêa Fanzeres, of the Native Amazonia Operation (OPAN, Operação Amazônia Nativa), an NGO that works with indigenous groups, organised the October gathering. She said that OPAN had deliberately chosen to hold the event in this square: 'All the people taking part in the festival live in the region. They are people who have been made invisible, people who suffer prejudice, people excluded from urban life. It was really daring of us to bring these people to a public square, to a square called the Square of the Colonisers'.

The 'history that began' alluded to on the Juara monument plaque commenced thousands of miles to the south during the country's dictatorship (1964–1985) when numerous rural families lost their livelihoods. There were many reasons for this: farming was becoming

Photo 1.1 A Munduruku Indian listens attentively during the Third Juruena Vivo Festival. Photo by Thais Borges

mechanized and required fewer labourers; the building of hydroelectric dams was forcing families to leave their homes to make way for reservoirs; and peasant plots were becoming too small for the land to be further divided among all the sons. As the government refused to carry out agrarian reform, these landless families could not be settled in their home states, and many were prepared to migrate thousands of miles north to gain a plot of land in the very different world of the Amazon frontier. While opposed to agrarian reform in the south and north-east, the military government was prepared to back land colonisation programmes in the 'empty' north and to provide 'land for the landless' in these schemes. It divided up swathes of land in the northern part of Mato Grosso state among just a few favoured owners: Juara, for example, was given to Zé Paraná; Sinop to Énio Pipino; Alta Floresta to Ariosto da Riva; and so on. These owners then sold the land on to small farmers, becoming very rich in the process. The military government also launched initiatives to encourage large companies to set up cattle ranches. As the plaque inscription notes approvingly, these settlers who 'began history' set about felling and burning the forest and planting crops. In the beginning, these colonising families found everything hard – the strange climate, the infertile soil, the lack of hospitals and schools, and the absence of government support. Many returned home but, as they say in the region, 'the pig-headed remained'.

Photo 1.2 The Statue of the Coloniser.
Photo by Thais Borges

But the alien conditions weren't the only problem. The settlers soon ran up against a huge governmental lie: the authorities had promised 'a land without people for a people without land', but the land was far from empty. In actual fact, indigenous people and traditional rubber tapping communities had long lived in the forests and on the river shores that were sold to the outsiders. Serious land and livelihood conflicts quickly erupted between newcomers seeking to develop the land and the progressively marginalised indigenous and traditional people who already lived and worked there. Occurring in remote areas, the conflicts were almost always hidden from the public eye.

In truth, until the progressive 1988 Brazilian Constitution was promulgated the indigenous people struggled for their very existence, for under previous legislation the Indians were allowed to stay on their land only until they were 'assimilated' into national society. Even though they have won far greater rights today, their centuries-long struggle is unrelenting and they have continued to lose land all over Brazil. As will be discussed later, from mid-2016, after the impeachment of President Dilma Rousseff, the new government of Michel Temer launched an extraordinary onslaught on indigenous rights, unprecedented since the return to civilian rule in 1985.

Escalating conflict

In the Mato Grosso part of the Tapajós basin, Indians today are often confined to shrinking 'islands': indigenous zones tentatively guaranteed by the government. As became clear from the impassioned testimonies at the festival, indigenous land all over the region is increasingly threatened by agribusiness's ambitious new infrastructure plans, by large mining projects, and by government schemes to delay and deny indigenous territorial demarcation.

But it is not only Indians who are in trouble. Landless peasants, who had migrated slowly into the region in earlier centuries, flocked to the Amazon in larger numbers in the early years of the 21st century, hopeful that the newly elected, left-wing Workers' Party (PT, Partido dos Trabalhadores) government would deliver on its pledge to carry out an extensive programme of agrarian reform, particularly in the Amazon. But the government broke its word, and many landless families had to fend for themselves, squatting on the land. Today they, along with Indians and traditional communities, are clinging to the land as first land grabbers, then cattle ranches, and then extensive soya plantation monocultures – mostly in the hands of wealthy, large-scale farmers – march deeper into the Amazon forest from both

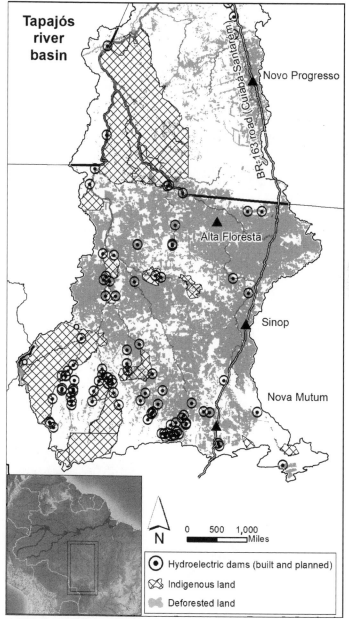

Map 1.1 Indigenous land, deforested land and planned and built hydroelectric dams in the Tapajós basin in Mato Grosso state.
Map by Maurício Torres

Mato Grosso in the south and Rondônia and Acre in the west. This collision of livelihood and lifestyle has resulted in violence and assassination. The state of Pará has become Brazil's most violent state, with 541 murders as a result of land conflicts, a third of the national total, recorded from 1985 to 2016 (Niklas, 2017).

Instead of responding with law enforcement, the government has sometimes tried to minimise and normalise the violence. At the UN Climate Conference in Marrakesh, Morocco, in November 2016, Brazil's Agriculture Minister, Blairo Maggi, himself one of the world's largest soya farmers, attributed the rising number of violent deaths to 'problems of personal relationships' (Amaral, 2016). Human rights activists take a different view, seeing the current violence as a conflict over land use, property, and culture. Fernanda Moreira, from the Catholic Church's Indigenous Missionary Council (CIMI, Conselho Indigenista Missionário) said: 'While the frightening level of violence in the countryside against Indians, peasant families, and leaders of social movements indicates the ethnocide character of these struggles, it also demonstrates the intensity with which these people are resisting'. This determination to fight back was the theme of many of the presentations at the Juruena Vivo Festival.

While there, we were invited by a Munduruku Indian, Cândido Waro, to visit his village – the Teles Pires village – on the Teles Pires river. Knowing that such invitations are not easy to come by, we changed plans and arranged to meet some Munduruku Indians at Porto do Meio, a three-hour drive from the town of Alta Floresta, for them to take us in a canoe with an outboard engine down the Teles Pires river to their village. It took us a day to make the trip and we occasionally had to get out of the canoe to walk down the river's rapids, but we reached the village without mishap.

References

All web references were checked and still available in June/July 2018 unless otherwise stated.

Amaral, A.C. (2016) '"Problemas de relacionamento" matam ambientalistas, diz ministro da Agricultura', *Folha de S. Paulo* [online] <http://www1.folha.uol.com.br/ambiente/2016/11/1833205-problemas-de-relacionamento-matam-ambientalistas-diz-ministro.shtml>

Niklas, J. (2017) 'Pará tem 30 per cent das mortes em conflitos por terra no Brasil', *O Globo* [website] <http://blogs.oglobo.globo.com/na-base-dos-dados/post/estado-mais-violento-para-tem-30-das-mortes-em-conflitos-por-terra-no-brasil.html>

CHAPTER 2
Dynamiting heaven

Description of life in the Munduruku indigenous village of Teles Pires, whose way of life and cosmology have been seriously damaged by the nearby construction of two hydroelectric dams, Teles Pires and São Manoel, on the Teles Pires river, one of the two 'legs' of the Tapajós river.

'It is a time of death. The Munduruku will start dying. They will have accidents. Even simple accidents will lead to death. Lightning will strike and kill an Indian. A branch will fall from a tree and kill an Indian. It's not chance. It's all because the government interfered with a sacred site'.

Krixi Biwūn (or Valmira Krixi Munduruku, as she was baptised) says this with authority. She is a respected Munduruku warrior living in the village of Teles Pires beside the river of the same name on the border between the Brazilian states of Mato Grosso and Pará. A well-built woman, she wears a traditional skirt made of straw, with necklaces fashioned from forest nuts around her neck. Though she is over 60, her long, straight, jet-black hair doesn't have a single white strand. She speaks to us with great confidence about subjects ranging from the old stories of her people to the plant-based concoctions in which young girls must bathe in order to transform themselves into warriors. She is a leader and a sage, and much esteemed in the village.

The sacred site she speaks about is a stretch of rapids, known in the indigenous language as *Paribixexe* and in Portuguese as *Sete Quedas* (Seven Rapids), located along the Teles Pires river. It is a sacred site for all the Munduruku. In 2013, the federal government gave the go-ahead to the consortium responsible for the construction of a large, 1.8-megawatt hydroelectric power station, called Teles Pires, to dynamite the rapids in order to make way for the dam. Later that year, the companies blew up *Sete Quedas* with explosives, and in so doing also destroyed a sacred sanctuary inhabited, in the cosmology of the region's indigenous people, by spirits after death – the equivalent of the Christian heaven.

The destruction of the sacred rapids was a lethal blow for the Indians: 'The dynamiting of sacred sites is the end of religion and

Photo 2.1 Valmira Krixi Munduruku.
Photo by Maurício Torres

Photo 2.2 The Teles Pires hydroelectric dam under construction.
Photo by Brent Millikan/International Rivers

the end of culture. It is the end of the Munduruku people. When they dynamited the rapids, they dynamited the Mother of the Fish and the Mother of the Animals we hunt. So these fish and these animals will die. All that we are involved with will die. So this is the end of the Munduruku', says a mournful indigenous elder, Eurico Krixi

Munduruku. The message Krixi Biwün delivers is equally chilling: 'We will die, and in our spirit too'. It is double annihilation, in life and in death.

In all, more than 13,000 Munduruku Indians live in 112 villages today, mainly along the upper reaches of the Tapajós river and its tributaries, including the Teles Pires. This indigenous group once occupied and held dominion over such an extensive Amazonian region that 'in colonial Brazil, the whole of the Tapajós river basin was known by the Europeans as Mundurukânia', explains Bruna Rocha, a lecturer in archaeology at the Federal University of the West of Pará. The sudden explosion of rubber tapping across Amazonia during the second half of the 19th century shattered the power of Mundurukânia and deprived the Munduruku of most of their territory. 'They kept fragments of their old territory in the lower Tapajós and larger areas in the upper reaches of the river, but even so it was only a fraction of what they occupied in the past', says Rocha.

Now even these fragments are being seriously affected by the hydroelectric power stations being built around them. Of the more than 40 big dams proposed for the Tapajós basin, four are already under construction or completed on the Teles Pires river, one of the two legs of the Amazon's Tapajós tributary. These dams are all key to a proposed industrial waterway, created by dredging the rivers and dynamiting the rapids, that would transport soya north along the Teles Pires and Tapajós rivers from Mato Grosso state, then east along the Amazon to the coast for export, mostly to China.

A faith fundamental to existence

The 90 families in Teles Pires village love talking about the past, a time, they say, when they could roam at will through their immense territory to hunt and harvest from the forest. However, for at least two centuries and possibly longer, they have lived in a fixed abode. But they still collect many products from the forest – seeds, tree bark, fibres, timber, fruit, and others – and use them to build their houses, to feed themselves, to make spears for hunting, and to concoct herbal remedies. Their territory – the Indigenous Territory of Kayabi – which they share, not always happily, with the Apiaká and Kayabi people, was designated indigenous land in 2004. Bizarrely, the sacred site of *Sete Quedas* was left just outside its legal limits. Although it may not have appeared important at the time, this oversight was to have tragic consequences for the Indians.

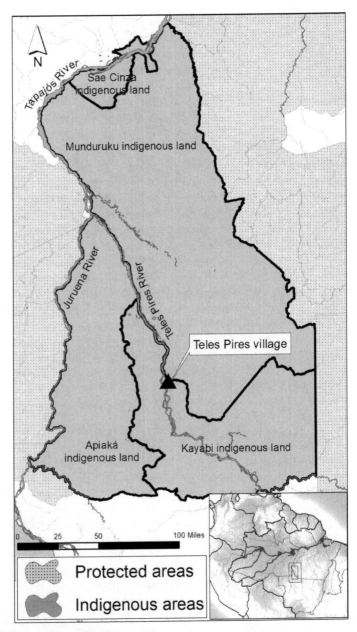

Map 2.1 Location of Teles Pires village.
Map by Maurício Torres

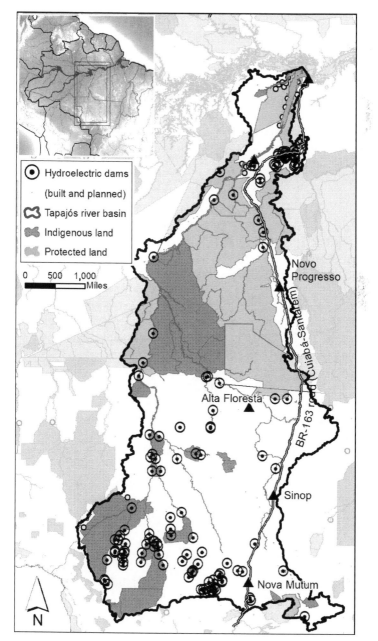

Map 2.2 Hydroelectric dams, indigenous land and protected land in the Tapajós basin.
Map by Mauricio Torres

Over the centuries, the Munduruku have changed as the world around them has changed, a process that intensified after they made contact with white society in the 18th century. On some occasions, they have readily incorporated new technological and social elements into their culture. The British Museum has a very traditional Munduruku waistband, probably fashioned in the late 19th century, which utilises cotton fabric imported from Europe. The Indians must have realised that cotton fabric was a useful alternative to the textiles they made from forest products, and they happily incorporated it into the decorative garment.

Today that custom continues. Almost all young people have mobile phones and, like urban Brazilians, delight in all they can do with them. But at times the Munduruku find, just as we do, that modern technology can go wrong, with frustrating results. For example, they installed an artesian well in Teles Pires village and now have running water in their houses. Except when the system breaks down, that is, which happens not infrequently. During the four days of our visit, there was no water as the pump had stopped working.

Franciscan friars have had a mission (*Missão Cururu*) in the heart of Munduruku territory for over a century, and Christianity has left its mark. The Munduruku say, for instance, that the creator of the world, the warrior Karosakaybu, fashioned everyone and everything 'in his own image and likeness', a direct quote from the Bible. Even so, the Indians have a strong ethnic identity, which they fiercely protect. When we asked to film them they said yes, but many insisted on speaking their own language on camera, even though they often could speak Portuguese better than our translator. Moreover, their cosmology is rock-solid and present in all aspects of their everyday life; every Indian to whom we spoke shared Krixi Biwūn's belief in the hereafter, and the importance of the sacred sites in guaranteeing their life after death. This fundamental faith is essential to their existence, which is why they now feel so distraught.

The dams the people didn't want

According to Convention 169 of the International Labour Organisation (ILO), national governments are obliged to consult directly with indigenous groups before launching any project that will affect their well-being. Brazil is a signatory of this agreement, so how is it possible that indigenous sacred sites were demolished on the Teles Pires river

Photo 2.3 Munduruku warriors.
Photo by Maurício Torres

to make way for Amazon dams? The answer is clear, according to Brent Millikan, Amazon Programme Director for International Rivers: the government failed to carry out the consultations mandated by the convention.

In 2011, after an epic battle, the government got the go-ahead for the building of the giant Belo Monte hydroelectric dam on the Xingu river, another major Amazon tributary, and it turned its attention to its next hydroelectric target in Amazonia – the Teles Pires river. 'It moved quickly and stealthily to build four dams on this river simultaneously. Two are close to the territory of indigenous people – the Teles Pires and São Manoel. The São Manoel dam is located 300 metres from the federally demarcated border of the Indigenous Territory of Kayabi, where the Munduruku, Kayabi, and Apiaká live', said Millikan. The sacred site of *Sete Quedas*, just outside the boundary of the indigenous territory, lay in the way of the São Manoel dam, he added, so the government quietly authorised its destruction.

Unlike the indigenous struggle to halt the Belo Monte mega-dam, which was extensively covered by the Brazilian and international press, 'the attempts made by the Munduruku and other indigenous peoples to stop the Teles Pires projects were ignored', Millikan continues. 'This was due to various factors: their geographic isolation; the fact that the dams were less grandiose than Belo Monte; the speed at which the government was moving; the very limited involvement of civil society groups, who generally help threatened groups; and so on'.

Even so, the government went through the motions of consulting with the indigenous population and other local inhabitants. On 6 October 2010, it announced in the official gazette that it had received the environmental impact study for the Teles Pires dam from the Brazilian Institute of the Environment and Renewable Natural Resources (IBAMA, Instituto Brasileiro do Meio Ambiente e dos Recursos Naturais Renováveis), and that the public had 45 days in which to request an *audiência pública* (public hearing) at which they could raise questions about the dam. A hearing was in fact held on 23 November 2010 in the town of Jacareacanga, Pará. Although the event was organised in a very formal way, quite alien to indigenous culture, contributions from 24 people, almost all of them indigenous, were permitted. According to the Federal Public Ministry (MPF, Ministério Público Federal), an independent body of federal prosecutors, every speaker expressed opposition to the dam. Even so, the dam went ahead. In time, the Munduruku began to feel that these hearings, held also for the other dams planned for the river, were mere box-ticking events, where they had no chance of affecting the outcome. They became increasingly reluctant to take part.

Although the Munduruku were always opposed to the dams, they were ill-prepared for the scale of the damage they have suffered. Cacique Disma Muõ told us: 'The government didn't inform us. The government always spoke of the good things that would happen. They didn't tell us about the bad things'. When they protested, they were told: 'The land belongs to the government, not to the Indians.

Box 2.1 MPF (Federal Public Ministry)

The Federal Public Ministry is an organ of public power, but it is autonomous from the other structures of the state and has its own budget. It does not belong to any of the three powers (executive, legislative, and judiciary).

The MPF defends citizens against abuses and omissions committed by the public powers and also defends public assets from assault by individuals of bad faith. It is tasked with defending citizens' social and individual rights (to life, dignity, freedom, and so on). It operates at the federal level in cases governed by the constitution and by federal laws, whenever the question involves public interest, either because of the parties involved or because of the issue. Among its main areas of expertise is combatting corruption and defending the rights of indigenous and tribal populations.

There is no way the Indians can prevent the dams'. This is, at best, a half-truth. Although indigenous territory belongs to the Brazilian state, the indigenous people have the right under the Brazilian Constitution to the exclusive and perpetual use of this land. Moreover, as has already been pointed out, the ILO's Convention 169 says that indigenous groups must be consulted if they will suffer an impact 'from plans for the overall economic development of the areas they inhabit', even if the cause of the impact is located outside their land. Rodrigo Oliveira, an MPF adviser in Santarém, made this clear in an interview he gave us: 'As it was evident before the dams were licensed that the Munduruku and other communities would be affected, the Brazilian government had the obligation to consult these groups in a full and informed way in accordance with the ILO's Convention 169'. And it didn't.

The Brazilian government repeatedly claimed that its public hearings amounted to the free, prior, and informed consultation required by the ILO, but the MPF challenged this. It sued the Brazilian government and, on several occasions, it won, and federal court rulings halted work on the dam. However, unfortunately for the Munduruku and other local indigenous groups, each time the MPF won in a lower court, the powerful interests of the energy sector – both within government and outside it – had the decision overturned in a higher court. This was largely possible because the Workers' Party government (in office 2003–16) had revived a legal instrument known as *Suspensão de Segurança* (Suspension of Security), which was instituted and widely used by Brazil's military dictatorship (1964–85). It allows any judicial decision, even when based on sound legal principles, to be reversed in a higher court without further legal argument, using a trump card that simply invokes national security, public order, or national economy.

The use of the *Suspensão de Segurança* instrument can be challenged – and has been challenged by the MPF – but it will take years, probably decades, for the challenge to be heard by the Supreme Federal Court. Even if the MPF eventually wins, by then the dams will be up and running – a fait accompli. The Prosecutor Luís de Camões Lima Boaventura told us: 'Figures collected by the MPF show that, just with respect to the hydroelectric dams in the Teles Pires–Tapajós basin, we were victorious in 80 per cent of the actions we took, but all of the rulings in our favour were reversed by suspensions'. According to Prosecutor Boaventura, the root of the problem is that the Brazilian authorities have always adopted a colonial mentality towards the Amazon, wanting to plunder its resources for the benefit of the metropolis, in this case the country's political and business centre. 'I would say that Amazonia hasn't been seen as a territory to be conquered. Rather, it's been seen as a territory to be pillaged. Predation is the norm'.

Instead of democratically engaging the Munduruku and discussing the various options for the future of the Tapajós region with them, federal authorities imposed the dams without debate. The Teles Pires dam was built in record time – 41 months – and is already operating. In January 2018, the National Agency for Electric Energy (ANEEL, Agência Nacional de Energia Elétrica) authorised the São Manoel dam to begin operations, in the midst of vociferous protests from the Munduruku.

Almost every week now, local indigenous villages feel another impact from these monster projects. The Indians say that the building of the São Manoel dam made the river dirty, more silted, and turbid. Although their claims have not been investigated, there seems little doubt that the aquatic life of the river will suffer significant long-term harm, as we discuss later. This is serious for a people whose diet consists largely of fish. In November 2016, crisis came in the form of an oil spill on the river, possibly originating at the dam construction site, which deprived some villages of drinking water.

We will have to pay the price

The destruction of the sacred *Paribixexe* rapids was not the only blow inflicted on the Munduruku by the consortium building the São Manoel dam. Workers also removed 12 funeral urns and archaeological artefacts from a nearby site, a violation of sacred tradition that has done further spiritual harm. Cacique Disma Mou, who is also a shaman, explains: 'We kept arrows, clubs, ceramics there, all buried under the ground in urns, all sacred. Many were trophies, placed there when we were at war, travelling from region to region. Our ancestors chose this place to be sacred and now it is being destroyed by the dam'.

In an interview, Francisco Pugliese, an archaeologist from the University of São Paulo, told us that he had been horrified by the behaviour of the National Institute of Historic and Artistic Heritage (IPHAN, Instituto do Patrimônio Histórico e Artístico Nacional), the body in charge of the protection of archaeological sites. In his view, the institute had broken the law by exempting the hydroelectric company from the obligation to work with the Munduruku in order to work out the best way of protecting their sacred site. To make the situation even worse, he went on, IPHAN had decided that, as the urns and other material were discovered outside the boundary of the indigenous reserve, they were the property of the government and should be sent to a museum. 'Imagine what it's like for a traditional people to see its ancestors taken to a place with which it has no emotional link and which it has never visited', he said. 'It's within this perverse logic of dispossession that archaeological research takes place in the context of the implementation of a dam. It exacerbates the process of expropriation and the destruction of the cultural references of the people, and it reinforces the process of genocide being inflicted on the original inhabitants of the Amazon basin', he concluded. We requested an interview with IPHAN but were not granted one.

The elder Eurico Krixi Munduruku finds it painful to describe what this sacrilege means for the people: 'Those urns should never have been touched. And it's not the white man who will pay for this. It is us, the living Munduruku, who will have to pay, in the form of accidents, in the form of death.... Our ancestors left them there for us to protect. It was our duty and we have failed. And now we, the Munduruku, will have to pay the price'. This was clearly demonstrated in the aftermath of a 2012 federal police operation known as Operation El Dorado, during which an Indian was killed, which will be described in the next chapter. Krixi Biwün, the sister of the man killed, told us that her brother's spirit is still suffering: 'He went to *Paribixexe* [*Sete Quedas*] because, when people die, that is where our ancestors take them so that they can live there. But now *Paribixexe* is destroyed and he is in agony'.

The ethnocide continues

Is there a way forward for the Munduruku people, a way that the perceived blasphemy perpetrated by the consortium and federal government can be reversed? Everyone we talked to in the village is certain of one thing: that, as long as the urns and other artefacts stay outside a sacred site, one catastrophe will follow another and even small wounds will cause death. But it is not simply a case of returning the urns to the Indians so they can rebury them. 'They can't give the urns back to us', explains Krixi Biwün. 'We can't touch them. They have to return them to a sacred place [without us]'. The urns are currently in the Museum of Natural History in the town of Alta Floresta.

The shamans, who in late 2017 carried out a ritual near them, have made it clear to the authorities that they want to choose where and how the reburial occurs. Even if the holy relics are eventually returned to a sacred place in one of the rapids along the Teles Pires river, that respite is likely to be short-lived. The next step in the opening up of the region to agribusiness and mining is to turn the Teles Pires into an industrial waterway, building dams, reservoirs, canals, and locks. This will mean dredging the river and destroying all the river's rapids, leaving no sacred sites.

The indefatigable MPF has carried on fighting. In December 2017, it won another victory in the courts, with a judge ruling that the licence for the installation of the Teles Pires dam – granted by the environmental agency, IBAMA – was invalid because of the failure to consult the Indians. Once again, however, this court order is unlikely to be enforced because it will be reversed by a higher court using the Suspension of Security instrument. Indeed, no judicial decision regarding the dams will be respected by the government until the case is judged by the Supreme Federal Tribunal, which may well take decades. In practical terms, what the tribunal decides will be irrelevant, for both the Teles Pires and the São Manoel dams are already operational.

The Indians are outraged by the lack of respect with which they are being treated. A statement issued jointly by the Munduruku, Kayabi, and Apiaká in 2011, and quoted in the book-length report, *Ocekadi* (see Box 2.2), asks: 'What would the white man say if we built our villages on the top of his buildings, his holy places, and his cemeteries?' It is, the Munduruku are saying, the equivalent of razing St Peters in Rome to construct a nuclear power plant, or digging up your grandmother's grave to build a parking lot.

In recent years the indigenous people have increasingly resorted to direct action. In October 2017, about 80 Munduruku warriors, men and women, some of whom had spent days travelling to the Teles Pires village from all over the Tapajós river basin, tried to occupy the São

---

Box 2.2 *Ocekadi*

Ocekadi is a word from the Munduruku language. When asked what it means, Munduruku Indians give slightly different, but always highly significant, answers: 'the river of our people'; 'our river'; 'the river of the Munduruku'; and so on. Invariably, they point to the river. It is their word for the Tapajós river. It was white people who called it the Tapajós, referring to an indigenous people, now extinct, who once lived along the river.

Manoel dam. The authorities had been tipped off and the Munduruku faced a barrage of armed Public Security National Force policemen, specially flown in, and were met by tear gas and flash bombs. Even so, the action brought some success: the construction company has at least engaged in talks with the shamans to determine where and how the sacred urns will be reburied.

The researcher Rosamaria Loures, who has been studying Munduruku opposition to the hydroelectric projects, told us that their experience reveals one of the weaknesses of Brazilian society: 'The nation state has established a hierarchy of values based on criteria like class, colour, and ethnic origin. In this categorisation, certain groups count less and can be simply crushed', she explains. A Munduruku Indian, Marcelo, who comes from an indigenous territory near the town of Juara and has spent time in towns furthering his education, expressed a similar notion in graphic terms: 'The ethnocide continues, in the way people look at us, the way they want us to be like them, subjugating our organisations, the way they tell us that our religion isn't worth anything, that theirs is what matters, the way they tell us our behaviour is wrong. They are obliterating the identity of the Indian as a human being'.

While we were in Teles Pires village, we were given information, never before revealed, about the invasion of the village by the federal police in 2012, during which an Indian was killed and several others seriously wounded. In the next chapter, we will describe in some detail this operation, which has left the Indians traumatised.

CHAPTER 3
Terror comes to the Teles Pires

First full account of the joint government operation, carried out in November 2012 in the Munduruku village of Teles Pires, to combat gold mining. Known as Operation El Dorado, it not only led to the death of one Indian and to the maiming of others, but shook to the core the Munduruku's trust in the authorities to the core.

Pariwat in the Munduruku language means both non-Indian and enemy. Perhaps if those in charge of Operation El Dorado had known this word, they might have carefully considered the proud warlike character of the Munduruku people, and their complex, troubled relationship with the white world. Instead, the authorities ordered a group of heavily-armed, ill-prepared men into the indigenous territory, where language, cosmology, political and legal systems, values, and even ways of thinking, are very different. All with predictable results: the federal raid on an Amazon indigenous village went terribly wrong. One Munduruku Indian was shot dead, others still suffer from debilitating wounds, and the confrontation has also done profound, long-term damage to relations between the Munduruku nation and the Brazilian state. Iandra Waro Munduruku remembers: 'The police arrived at our house and forced their way in. They searched the whole house. With their machine guns pointing at us, they told us to put our hands on our head and to leave the house. I was calling on them to calm down'. She was dumbfounded: 'We never imagined a federal policeman doing this to us. We trusted them a lot. We thought the federal police were our friend'.

The story of that day's events, hidden by an apparent police cover-up and never fully told in the press, is presented here. Our reporting has resulted in the MPF bringing a judicial action against the government for collective moral damage.

In search of Amazon gold

As with many indigenous conflicts during Latin America's history, Operation El Dorado was all about gold. It was launched in November 2012,

Photo 3.1 Iandra Waro Munduruku.
Photo by Thais Borges

when a federal judge in Cuiabá ordered the destruction of barges illegally dredging for gold in the indigenous land of the Munduruku, Apiaká, and Kayabi peoples living along the Teles Pires river. Federal Police Officer Antônio Carlos Moriel Sanchez headed up a National Public Security Force detachment to do the job. Representatives from Brazil's Indian agency, FUNAI (Fundação Nacional do Índio - National Indian Foundation (Brazil)) and IBAMA, the environmental agency, also took part.

In an explanatory note issued just after the violent raid, the federal police named their objective: to dismantle a criminal scheme in which legitimate companies, known as DTVMs (Distribuidora de Títulos e Valores Mobiliários – Securities Distribution Companies), illegally bought up gold in the indigenous territory (Polícia Federal, 2012). These companies, acting as middlemen on Brazil's financial and capital markets, reportedly served as money laundering platforms, concealing the gold's illegal origin, with highly profitable results for investors: more than R$150 m (US$46 m) in 10 months.

What made this apparently praiseworthy operation problematic was that it didn't just go after the companies, but also set about cutting off the gold at its source – with the police destroying the gold mining barges. Though the mining itself was illegal, it had gone on peacefully for many years in the Teles Pires village and was making a significant contribution to the indigenous economy, providing a cash income without which they would find it difficult to survive in the modern world. Indeed, the Munduruku have mined gold since the 18th century. From the 1970s onward, after it was discovered that the world's largest gold deposits lay under their land, the Indians have played a more active role in its management, aware that they ran a risk of their territory being invaded by swarms of autonomous gold miners. All this meant that, whether he knew it or not, when the Cuiabá judge ordered an end to gold mining in the Tapajós basin, he was attacking a long-time source of income for the Teles Pires village, which the indigenous people saw as legitimate.

When in Mundurukânia

Though much reduced in size and power today, Mundurukânia remains its own world with its own rules and rituals – customs that the federal police and FUNAI apparently failed to consider. One of the targeted gold mining barges operating near the village of Teles Pires was owned by a Munduruku Indian named Camaleão, who lived in a neighbouring village, and with whom the Teles Pires people had a close relationship (some local Indians even occasionally worked on the barge).

The federal officials' first mistake: the police and FUNAI held a five-hour meeting with the Teles Pires Munduruku on 6 November 2012, and those in attendance agreed that the barge would be destroyed. The authorities considered this meeting to be conclusive. The Munduruku did not. Within their tradition, agreement requires many meetings, with every community member. That's because, as anyone who has spent time in a Munduruku village knows, the community isn't hierarchical but is horizontally organised. Nothing is ever decided by the vote of a few. Consensus must be reached for action to occur – no matter how long it takes.

Any person arriving in a Munduruku village must follow rigorous protocol, as we learned on our trip to Teles Pires in November 2016. We had been invited in advance to visit, and arrived as expected, tired after a long river trip. Still, we had to wait on the quayside while a young warrior announced us to the cacique and requested our entry to the village. After a few minutes, the man returned and took us to the communal hut for the first of many meetings negotiating our journalistic goals.

We were introduced to the cacique, the vice-cacique, and other Indians waiting to receive the *pariwat*. They had all donned ceremonial clothes for our visit – the women in straw skirts, their faces painted with designs signifying the tail of a bird known as a *ukpisuesue*; the men hefting bows and arrows, their bodies painted with lozenge shapes resembling the shell of a *jabutí* (turtle), a creature which has gained mythical importance for the Munduruku, as it defeats its powerful enemies through clever stratagems. At last, we were guided to our room to sleep, and the next day awoke to a bell, calling us to a collective breakfast. Then more speeches. We worked out a programme for our visit, but it wasn't adhered to and we often found out quite suddenly that a new activity had been arranged.

The only constants were the daily meetings, at breakfast and in the evening. We gradually discovered that although our hosts often deviated from the agreed programme, that programme was still important: it functioned as a prescribed ritual. (If that seems strange, consider how a Munduruku warrior would respond to the formal protocol surrounding a visit to Buckingham Palace or the White House). We soon understood that not to follow protocol was to commit a serious misdemeanour. Indeed, it was precisely these rituals that the Brazilian state attempted to crush in its centuries-long effort to assimilate the many indigenous nations into so-called national society.

As Erika Yamada, a UN specialist on the rights of indigenous people, later told us, Brazilian attitudes showing lack of respect for indigenous rituals remain prevalent. In her view, the way in which the Brazilian state routinely ignores indigenous customs is 'a form of state racism, which needs to be given serious attention if the violence and discrimination are to be ended and Brazil turned into a country which recognises and respects diversity without discrimination'.

A day of terror

The federal police trampled on these protocols during Operation El Dorado, despite the fact that the officer in charge, Antônio Carlos Moriel Sanchez, had six years of experience leading the police unit for preventing crimes against indigenous communities. Early on the morning of 7 November 2012, the day following the first Munduruku meeting, armed police arrived abruptly by helicopter and speedboat, aiming to proceed immediately to destroy the gold mining barge. The Indians, who had been expecting another round of talks, were horrified.

Iandra Waro Munduruku, the daughter of the then cacique, recalls: 'We were told to get ready for this visit, to prepare ourselves, just as you see us here, prepared for you [in ritual garb].... They told us we were going to have a meeting with them. So we came, but instead we were treated to this terror. It was a day of terror'. In a disastrous clash of cultures, the federal police misinterpreted the Indians' wearing of ceremonial clothes. In their explanatory note, the police erroneously claim that the Munduruku had prepared an ambush, where 'over 100 Indians in war paint attacked, with firearms and bows and arrows, about 35 policemen'.

The reference to firearms appears to be wrong too: according to a report drawn up by the MPF and also according to the Indians we spoke to, none of the Munduruku had weapons apart from their ceremonial bows and arrows. The note also refers to 'authorised telephone recordings', which proved that 'an attack on the police was planned'. Not one of these recordings has been produced. The note also fails to mention the fact that an Indian was shot and killed. The federal police did not reply to our request for an interview.

The disrespectful invasion of the village by the federal police angered the community. Then, according to the MPF, things escalated. Camaleão, the barge owner – probably furious at the prospect of losing his investment, which was worth up to half a million dollars – approached officer Sánchez and told him to stop destroying his property. Sánchez reportedly pushed Camaleão, who then collided with another Indian, Adenilson Krixi Munduruku. According to Indian witnesses, Sánchez stumbled on the steep, slippery riverbank and fell into the river. Standing in water up to his waist, he then shot Adenilson three times in the leg so that he too fell into the water.

Adenilson's brother, Genivaldo Krixi Munduruku, takes up the story: 'I told them [the police] to stop, to keep calm.... My brother was already in the water, bleeding. He was struggling to get out of the water. I was trying to help him. He was pulling himself out. Then the officer shot him in the head. He lost consciousness. I've no doubt at all that [the police] wanted to kill him'. Subsequent examinations confirmed that Adenilson was killed by a shot to the nape of his neck. Or, in the words of the MPF, he was executed.

The killing triggered further violent police action. They began firing live ammunition and rubber bullets, and throwing tear gas bombs. The Indian warriors defended themselves by shooting arrows, wounding a few policemen. Several Indians were injured, a few seriously.

Genivaldo went on: 'I was dazed. So much shooting. So much smoke. My eyes were burning. I was almost blind. I found my son, a toddler, less than two years old. I picked him up and took him home'. Krixi Biwün, one of Adenilson's sisters and a highly respected female warrior, continues: 'I was hiding in the forest. The police were throwing bombs and the children were fleeing in terror. I almost died from fright. Nearly all my family was in the forest with me. And then I heard that my brother had been killed', she said, sobbing. 'I thought they were going to kill more people'.

Eurico Krixi Munduruku, an elderly Munduruku, relates his experience: 'I saw a lot of blood below the barge, it was the blood of our relative. I got frightened and started to leave. Then my arm got heavy and I couldn't run any more. It was a bullet that had hit my arm. My grandson helped me home'. Adenilson's wife, Ivete Saw, was toasting manioc flour when she heard that her husband had been killed: 'I could hear the bombs, the shooting, everything from the manioc hut. Then my daughter came and said: "Mummy, they've killed Daddy". I knocked over the manioc meal and it scattered on the floor. And then I started running toward the river. People said: "Don't go. You'll be killed". I said: "I must! I must!" But they held me back. If I'd gone, I'd have died with him'.

Most villagers retreated to their homes, but the police pursued them, knocking down doors and storming into every house. Danilo Krixi Munduruku, another of Adenilson's brothers, remembers: 'The police told us to leave our houses or they'd throw a bomb into them. The women came out, screaming with fear. They [the police] took us to the centre of the village. Pointing machine guns at us, they made us lie on the ground and then they handcuffed us. They said that if a policeman was killed, we'd all be killed. We lay there for hours. It was very hot and we were very thirsty'. Some Indians tried to record what was happening with their cell phones. The police seized all the phones they could find and destroyed the memory cards, but some Indians hid their phones, so some footage survived.

The police made all the men, including Iandra's father, put their hands on their heads and lie down. 'I kept saying: "But my father's the cacique! You have to treat him with respect!"' But it didn't make any difference. 'They treated them all like criminals. My grandfather, who was 86 years old, was treated like all the rest. I got very upset seeing

Photo 3.2 Edvaldo Moris Borô Munduruku shows his withered arm to LAB journalists. Photo by Maurício Torres

him dragged along the ground'. Edvaldo Moris Borô Munduruku was seriously hurt, with bullet shots in his back and his arm. He said that his arm was already splintered when the police came into his house but they twisted it further.

The police chased after Eurico Krixi: 'The federal police knocked down the door to my house. They forced their way in. They grabbed me, even though I was hurt, and threw me into the helicopter. They seized me as if they were taking me hostage. I began to feel very ill. I wanted water but they only gave me a little. I lost consciousness. I felt I was going to die'.

Aftermath

Seventeen men, including the wounded Eurico Krixi Munduruku, were taken prisoner and removed to a jail in Cuiabá, a large city they had never seen before. The men were disoriented, not knowing where they were, and fearful they would never be allowed back home. In interviews with us, two of the men said that they wanted to tell us what had really happened. While in custody, they had begun by telling the truth and blaming the police officer for the violence and for the death of Adenilson, but under police intimidation they changed their story.

Eliano Waro Munduruku explains: 'I've never said this before, but I'll say it now. We were told [by the police] to blame Camaleão [the indigenous leader who owned the barge]. We were told that if we told the truth, we'd be arrested, we wouldn't return to the village. We were so traumatised. We never believed that the federal police would do this to us. We trusted them. So we blamed Camaleão'.

Four years later, the horror of Operation El Dorado is still very real for the Indians. The remains of the exploded barge can still be seen at the quayside, a daily reminder of the terror they lived through. Some Indians have never recovered from their wounds. Edvaldo Moris Munduruku, whose arm was broken in two places, has suffered long-term effects: his forearm has atrophied and he can't move his fingers, so can no longer work the land. The elder, Eurico Krixi Munduruku, can't move his right arm: 'I can't fish anymore. I don't have any movement in my right arm, only in the left'. He can't even throw manioc flour into his mouth with his right hand, as all the other Indians do, but has to use a spoon, which he finds mortifying.

According to Genivaldo, his father never recovered from his son's death: 'The day after the operation, Adenilson's body appeared. It floated to the surface [of the river]. My father saw it and he's never recovered...He has gone silent and refuses to talk. He's still like that today'. Children are scared when they hear a helicopter overhead. People cry when they talk about the raid. The community

Photo 3.3 Eurico Krixi Munduruku.
Photo by Maurício Torres

has completely lost faith in FUNAI, which, they say, did nothing to protect them.

The federal police were shaken by the outcry following Adenilson's death. Operation El Dorado was halted and never resumed. Although police officer Antônio Carlos Moriel Sánchez has not been charged with any offence, we were told that he has been posted to Bolivia, where he carries out minor duties. We requested a phone interview with him to hear his version of events but were not given one.

Some in the village are beginning to recover. Valmira Krixi Munduruku says: 'It's taken me a long while to get over it and to get involved in the struggle again. But we Munduruku women are strong. We will fight against anything that is wrong. The creator of the world, Karosakaybu, made this law that the women would be strong, be warriors. We wash girls with a herb from the forest to make them strong'. However, it appeared to us as outsiders that the community would take a long time to regain its old confidence. Although there is no evidence that the authorities intended to weaken the Munduruku through Operation El Dorado, that has been one consequence.

Prosecuting the state

Hearing of our visit, MPF prosecutor Janaína Andrade de Sousa asked to see the video interviews we had filmed in the village, and on 17 November 2016 she decided to begin proceedings against the Brazilian state for the collective moral damage inflicted on the Munduruku Indians that day. It is highly unusual for a prosecutor to take such action on behalf of an indigenous community, and she is demanding a large compensation payment – R$10 m (US$2.9 m).

Unfortunately for the Munduruku, the blows suffered by the Indians in the Teles Pires village did not end with Operation El Dorado. As we described earlier, the consortium that were building the Teles Pires dam destroyed the very sacred site of *Sete Quedas* a few months later, causing more trauma. More assaults on the indigenous communities may be imminent, with the Temer government, National Congress, and agribusiness lobby (*Bancada Ruralista*) moving steadily toward approving a vast industrial waterway along the Teles Pires river. This commodity transportation route would destroy other sacred sites and disrupt the Munduruku's traditional lifestyle and livelihoods by ruining fishing grounds and bringing deforestation that would have a severe impact on hunting.

This may, however, be only the first of many modern assaults on the indigenous way of life. In the process of researching this article, we discovered that Vale S.A., one of the world's largest mining companies, has obtained mining rights for the soil beneath the Teles Pires village. Mining on indigenous land is currently forbidden under the Brazilian Constitution, but this could change rapidly if a new mining law already in congress, and supported by the powerful mining lobby, is approved. Vale S.A. is well known in Brazil for the callous way in which it has treated indigenous people in the past (Mattera, n.d.). It was also the parent company responsible for Brazil's worst environmental disaster, when the Fundão tailings dam collapsed in Mariana, Minas Gerais, in November 2015. A wave of toxic mud engulfed the village of Bento Rodrigues, killing 19 people and polluting the entire 440-mile course of the Rio Doce all the way to the Atlantic Ocean (Gonzalez, 2016).

While the Operation El Dorado raid shook Munduruku society to the core, the people remain united as a warrior nation. After all, they are the descendants of the great 'head choppers', known for their war-like behaviour until the start of the 20th century. And they have overcome many challenges in the past, surviving the coming of the rubber barons, land grabbers, and other *pariwat*. Today they stand firm, with their legion of male and female warriors, backed by the god of all creation, Karosakaybu. To our eyes, as visiting journalists, they seem ready and willing to face down the Brazilian government, the agribusiness lobby, and the dam builders.

We made the return journey up the Teles Pires river and back to the small town of Alta Floresta, where the company that built the Teles Pires dam has an office. We knew that they had won awards for the sustainability of their hydroelectric dam and we wanted to find out more.

References

All web references were checked and still available in June/July 2018 unless otherwise stated.

Gonzalez, J. (2016) 'One-year anniversary of Brazil dam disaster brings prosecutions', *Mongabay* [online] <https://news.mongabay.com/2016/11/one-year-anniversary-of-brazil-dam-disaster-brings-prosecutions/>

Mattera, P. (no date) 'Vale: Corporate rap Sheet', *Corporate Research Project* [website] <https://www.corp-research.org/vale>

Polícia Federal (2012), 'Nota à imprensa – Operação Eldorado', http://www.pf.gov.br/agencia/noticias/2012/novembro/nota-a-imprensa-operacao-eldorado

CHAPTER 4
An award for the dam builders

Despite the damage done by the Teles Pires hydroelectric scheme to the surrounding forest and indigenous communities, the builder and operator of the dam was given a Chico Mendes Award in 2014 for its 'responsible social and environmental management'. The granting of the award enraged many environmentalists, but the company says it strictly adhered to all the demands made on it by the government's environmental and indigenous agencies.

In April 2014, the Teles Pires Hydroelectric Company – builder and operator of Brazil's Teles Pires dam – was awarded a Green Certificate in the Responsible Social and Environmental Management category of the Chico Mendes Award, a prize named after the world-famous Brazilian social activist and eco-hero, who was assassinated in 1988 (IICM, 2014). An NGO called the Chico Mendes International Research and Social and Environmental Responsibility Institute (IICM, Instituto Internacional de Pesquisa e Responsabilidade Socioambiental Chico Mendes) had selected the winner. According to their website, the award goes to companies that provide Brazil with 'solutions to conflicts between development, social justice, and environmental equilibrium' (IICM, n.d.). The announcement of these awards 'is considered the most important socio-environmental event in Brazil', says the institute. In our trip to Teles Pires village, we had seen the enormous damage that the dynamiting of their most sacred site had done to the Munduruku Indians. Studies had also shown that, as so often happens when a big new project is undertaken in the Amazon, migrants had been attracted into the area and were damaging the forest (Locatelli, 2015). How could this company have won such an award?

The company maintains that it adhered scrupulously to the guidelines provided by the environmental agency, IBAMA, and that it cannot be blamed for environmental and social damage that occurred outside the strict confines of its land (Repórter Brasil, 2015). Átila Rocha, the company's Social Communication Co-ordinator, told us that they had carried out 19 tailor-made environmental programmes that ranged from monitoring the quality of the water in indigenous villages to the promotion of indigenous culture. The Chico Mendes Green Certificate, he said, recognizes the contribution the company makes, through its dams, to sustainable development and improvements in the life of the populations in the region around it.

This isn't the only green honour that has been lavished on the company. Two groups linked to the Brazilian energy sector – Power Brasil and the Incende Brasil Institute – awarded prizes to the firm, in 2014 and in 2016, for its innovation and commitment to social and environmental sustainability. The Teles Pires Hydroelectric Company also received important environmental recognition in 2012, when it requested and obtained Kyoto Protocol carbon credits (UNFCCC, n.d.). Under the UN's Clean Development Mechanism (CDM), hydroelectric dam projects in developing countries that reduce carbon dioxide emissions can earn these credits, which in turn can be sold to industrialised countries to help them to meet their emissions reduction targets.

But many social scientists feel that none of this compensates for the great damage that the dam is causing to the indigenous communities. In an interview with us, University of São Paulo Archaeologist Francisco Pugliese said he was angry but not surprised that a project that had destroyed an indigenous sacred site had won an award for social and environmental responsibility: 'This award goes against everything that you could expect from a prize that carries the name of Chico Mendes, and its consequences will be catastrophic if it is used as an example of social responsibility, rendering even dirtier and more lethal the production of energy by the hydroelectric dams that are planned or built in indigenous territory'.

The US$2-bn Teles Pires dam has an installed estimated capacity of 1,820 megawatts, making it the second largest hydropower project (after the Belo Monte mega-dam) of the Programme for the Acceleration of Growth (PAC, Programa de Aceleração do Crescimento) promulgated by President Luiz Inácio Lula da Silva. It was given a first phase environ-mental licence in 2010 and was built in record time, just 41 months. It began operating in November 2015, despite numerous protests and lawsuits launched against it, before and during construction, by indigenous and traditional communities, environmentalists, and the MPF.

The UN award of the carbon credits to the Teles Pires Hydroelectric Company came despite the fact that recent research has shown that newly built tropical dams, with their reservoirs full of rotting vegetation, produce significant amounts of methane, a greenhouse gas 20 times as potent as carbon dioxide. 'Various studies have shown that the emissions from hydroelectric dams in the Amazon are considerable in the first 10 years, which is the period that the carbon credits cover', commented Philip Fearnside, a scientist and an opponent of Amazon dams at the National Institute of Amazonian Research (INPA, Instituto Nacional de Pesquisas Amazônicas).

Inadequate assessments

Given so much public praise for the Teles Pires dam, one would perhaps expect that the project had been subjected to a thorough scientific appraisal of its potential impacts prior to the decision to construct it. But no such evaluation took place, said Brent Millikan, Amazon programme director for the NGO International Rivers. A long-time critic of the Brazilian government's rush to build so many Amazon dams, Millikan told us that: 'the political decision to build the Teles Pires dam came years before the technical, economic, and environmental viability studies were carried out'.

When those studies were finally carried out, care was taken, reports Millikan, to make sure that there were no surprises that would derail or slow the project. For instance, Leme Engenharia was one of the firms chosen to do the assessment. But Leme had a history of working with construction giant Odebrecht, helping it to build two dams (Capim Branco I and II) in the state of Minas Gerais. It also happens that Odebrecht was a key player in building the Teles Pires dam: it was both a minority shareholder in the Teles Pires Hydroelectric Company and part of the consortium chosen to build the dam. But the government never addressed the conflict of interest.

As with any major construction project, the studies carried out by Leme and other firms should have considered all potential project impacts, including negative effects on fisheries, aquatic and terrestrial ecosystems, biodiversity, traditional and indigenous communities, climate change, and more. None of the studies' findings led IBAMA to delay or redesign the construction process in any significant way. And much research simply wasn't carried out, or, when it was, the experts in charge did a slapdash job. Solange Arrolho, a lecturer at Mato Grosso State University, who is an expert on the fish in the Teles Pires river, told us: 'Most of those carrying out the impact studies were not from the region. They didn't go to fish markets. They scarcely talked to local fishermen or the local universities. I have been here for 25 years and have a larger collection of local fish than anyone else, yet the studies were carried out without anyone coming here to talk to me'.

According to Arrolho, the shortcomings of the studies have led to the environmental and social costs of the dams being seriously underestimated, not only in the case of Teles Pires but all over the Amazon region. 'When a project is planned – a road or a hydroelectric dam, for example – what do the assessment firms conclude? That it is viable, because they don't take into consideration the whole social and environmental process. The environmental and social impact they consider is tiny compared with the real one'.

A study published in *Nature* in June 2017 made a similar point (Latrubesse, 2017). The issue, say the study's authors, is that the impact studies for Amazonian river dams have focused mainly on the immediate area around the construction. 'Nobody considers the teleconnections', says lead author Edgardo Latrubesse, a professor at the Department of Geography and the Environment at the University of Texas, Austin. 'If I build the dam here, what is happening upstream, what is happening downstream? And if you build the dam in multiple places along a river, the impact is magnified. This isn't considered when they build the project' (Pierre-Louis, 2017). Ricardo Scoles, lecturer in ecology at the Federal University of the West of Pará, also concludes that the dams' impacts were routinely underestimated. 'There is no scientific basis for guaranteeing low social and environmental impacts when building a dam in a region of high social and environmental diversity, such as the Teles Pires basin', he declared flatly. 'The Tapajós–Xingu is a region with a high level of endemic species, and thus the potential impacts on the fauna will be severe and tend to be irreversible, given that many of the animals are only found in this bioregion'. For Scoles, 'it is highly irresponsible to interfere in the dynamic of the watercourses in southern Amazonia, a region already affected by local climatic changes, with a decline in rainfall and more prolonged droughts'.

Federal failings

Brazilian authorities weren't blind to the environmental issues being ignored and minimised during construction of the Teles Pires dam. At times, the technical staff within IBAMA and FUNAI balked at the reports they were receiving from the private companies doing the assessments. Indeed, there were several federal rows over the Teles Pires licensing process, according to Millikan. The Energy Research Company (EPE - Empresa de Pesquisas Energéticas), a federal body in charge of planning Brazil's energy supply, was outraged when IBAMA and FUNAI raised objections to the Teles Pires dam, even though it was their official duty to raise them. Conflict within FUNAI was particularly fierce. In December 2010, agency staff produced a detailed technical critique of the dam's environmental impact study, arguing that the indigenous portion had to be completely reformulated. But a few days later, the president of FUNAI, under intense pressure from the energy sector and from the office of Brazil's president, gave the go-ahead for the first phase of the dam. A week later, the tendering process was undertaken to decide which companies would build it.

The study irregularities didn't stop there. There were so many that, in August 2012, a federal judge declared that the impact studies carried out by the Teles Pires Hydroelectric Company were 'totally compromised and lacking in legality, for infringing the constitutional principles of public order, impartiality, and environmental morality' (Borges, 2012). He upheld a lower court ruling to immediately halt work on the dam. But his decision was soon overturned through the use of a judicial trump card, the *Suspensão de Segurança* power.

One of the few forums where there was some, albeit limited, public discussion about the possible impacts of the dam was in the public comments section of the UN CDM (UNFCCC Projects, n.d.). When the Teles Pires Hydroelectric Company was in the process of requesting credits in 2012, several bodies, both Brazilian and international, raised objections. Indigenous groups made strong complaints, with the Kayabi Indians warning of the impact that the construction of the dam would have on their spiritual life, as it would destroy *Sete Quedas*, the sacred site on a rapid on the Teles Pires river. In its response, the Teles Pires Hydroelectric Company claimed that 'currently [the site on the *Sete Quedas* rapids] is not an area that is frequented or used [by indigenous people]' (UNFCCC Projects, n.d.) and that it is not 'a location of sacred importance'. This is factually wrong. It had been known for many years that *Sete Quedas* was a sacred site and that the Indians did not visit it precisely because it was so sacred. The Munduruku had long warned that its destruction would have catastrophic consequences for them, spiritually and materially. But no one listened. The rapids were dynamited to make way for the dam and, sure enough, the Indians suffered a horrific impact, as we saw in our visit to the Teles Pires village described in earlier chapters.

Photo 4.1 Mato Grosso State University lecturer Solange Arrolho.
Photo by Thais Borges

Cumulative impacts

We asked fish expert Solange Arrolho about the observable impacts that the now completed dam has had on fish stocks. She explained that hurried construction had prevented the proper gathering of baseline data in advance of the project, making it impossible to do before and after assessments. But she could say with certainty that the project had affected fish migration: 'Before the dam was built, some fish, particularly large ones, migrated along the upper reaches of the Teles Pires, something that they cannot now do as the dam doesn't have a side channel that allows them to get past the plant', she said. But so far, bigger fish have survived. 'They are finding other places to reproduce downstream. But they will become more vulnerable, much easier to catch, as they are held in large quantities in front of the dam'. Her views were corroborated by Francisco Arruda Machado, widely known as *Chico Peixe* (Chico Fish), an environmental adviser to the MPF in Mato Grosso. In January 2016, he collected fish samples in the Verde river, a Teles Pires tributary upstream from the dam. 'In the past, I would collect 10–15 big fish, fish like the *matrinxã* or *curimbatá*, each about 2.5–3 kilos (5.5–6.6 pounds)', he said. 'This year I didn't catch a single one. This proves to me that the fish aren't managing to migrate up the river to spawn'.

The Munduruku Indians live downstream, so they shouldn't yet be affected by the disruption in migratory flow, but many complained to us on our visit to their villages that the fishery appears to be in decline. Sandro Waro Munduruku, a young leader, told us: 'There are far fewer fish. We don't catch as many as we used to before the dam was built. Shoals of fish are dying. We don't know how we are going to live in the future'. Arrolho explained the probable reason for the decline in fishery that the Indians have noted. With the building of the dam 'methane and other gases are produced through the decomposition of organic material. When these gases come to the surface, the water becomes more acid, the amount of oxygen declines, the [water] temperature increases.... The whole structure of the river is altered. The fish don't eat properly and there aren't enough nutrients for the reproductive processes. It's a big change'.

Those changes will worsen over time. 'The adverse impacts [of the dam] are cumulative', explained Arrolho. 'At the headwaters of the Teles Pires, there are a lot of large farms, with kilos and kilos of sediments, fertilisers, and herbicides running off into the river. The dam downstream now prevents these residues from dispersing and they will accumulate'. The consequences are predictable: 'It is like putting fertilisers into a bowl of water and then placing it in the sun. The water soon goes green with algae'. These consume the oxygen in the water, and aquatic life dies. 'Who pays for this environmental degradation? Fish *and* people', she concluded.

But according to Arrolho, the state government has shown little concern for the failing fishery. 'For many years, successive Mato Grosso governments have thought of Amazonian culture – which is a culture of river people, of people who know the importance of water – as a problem to be overcome', she said. 'For years, the state government even went so far as to deny that any part of the Amazon basin lay within its boundaries, though it accounts for 67 per cent of the state's territory'. And now this traditional Amazonian way of life is disappearing: 'Instead, we have this culture of electric energy, of grain production, of mining'. Arrolho is pessimistic about the future, fearing irreversible damage to the river's aquatic life, with 'the impacts of the dams tending to get worse in the medium and long term'.

Confronted with all these criticisms, the Teles Pires Hydroelectric Company has consistently pointed out that it has conformed with all the demands made on it by federal agencies, and that it has gone even further in terms of good practice. In a special issue of its company magazine, titled 'Teles Pires – Brazil's model hydroelectric project', Neoenergia, the main partner in the dam construction consortium, wrote that it had redesigned the original project 'to reduce further the environmental impacts, involving advanced techniques of sustainable engineering', and that 'compared with other hydro-dams, the project stands out for its high energy yield and low impact' (Repórter Brasil, 2015). In an interview with *Repórter Brasil*, the firm asserted that it was careful not to damage the forest when building the dam, lodging its 6,000 construction workers on the building site, just as if the company had been building an oil rig in the middle of the ocean (Repórter Brasil, 2015).

But the firm's green building efforts become largely irrelevant when measured against the dam's likely long-term impacts. No big dam has ever been built in the Brazilian Amazon without generating a large population influx, provoking wholesale deforestation. A similar effect is predictable for the Teles Pires river basin, especially when adding in the four other dams being built on the river. Yet, when *Repórter Brasil* asked the company to comment on the recent record level of deforestation (18,000 hectares) in the district around the dam, it had no answer except to claim that 'there is no way of establishing a connection between the increase in forest clearance and the arrival of the [hydroelectric dam] project' (Repórter Brasil, 2015).

Sharing responsibility

Even critics concede that the Teles Pires Hydroelectric Company itself is not responsible for initiating many of the dam's environmental and social impacts. After all, it was the government that decided to give the go-ahead to the project without adequate studies, to preclude an open public debate, and to resort to authoritarian acts, such as using the *Suspensão de Segurança* to get the dam built. Even so, critics find it hard to stomach that a prize bearing the name of Chico Mendes should be awarded to the Teles Pires Hydroelectric Company.

Francisco Pugliese noted that the award is a good example of how corporate activity and profits often outweigh social and environmental responsibility. 'If you look at the prize closely, you will see that it was given by a private institute linked to a very specific field of national economic power – which is not just active in Brazil, but in many countries of the world – the big construction companies'. Private institutions and major infrastructure companies, he pointed out, may paint themselves green, but that doesn't make them so.

By now, it was time to move on, to see for ourselves the soya plantations that had mushroomed in the north of Mato Grosso state and were being so criticised by indigenous and riverine communities and environmentalists. So we got into our pick-up and drove along the BR-163 highway to the town of Sinop, which lies at the heart of the new agribusiness empire.

References

All web references were checked and still available in June/July 2018 unless otherwise stated.

Borges, A. (2012) 'Estudo de impacto ambiental da usina Teles Pires é "nulo", aponta TRF', *Valor Econômico* [website] <http://www.valor.com.br/empresas/2786836/estudo-de-impacto-ambiental-da-usina-teles-pires-e-nulo-aponta-trf>

Grupo Neoenergia (2016) 'Teles Pires A Usina Modelo do Brasil', *Neoenergia* [online] <https://issuu.com/neoenergia/docs/revista_neo_energia-vfinal>

IICM (no date) Instituto Internacional de Pesquisa e Responsabilidade Socioambiental Chico Mendes <http://institutochicomendes.org.br>

IICM (2014) Instituto Internacional de Pesquisa e Responsabilidade Socioambiental Chico Mendes, Premiados de 2014, Categoria Gestão Socioambiental Responsável, Companhia Hidrelétrica Teles Pires <http://ambientes.ambientebrasil.com.br/educacao/premios_ambientais/premio_chico_mendes_de_meio_ambiente.html>

Latrubesse, E.M., Arima, E.Y., Dunne, T., Park, E., Baker, V.R., d'Horta, F.M., Wight, C., Wittmann, F., Zuanon, J., Baker, P.A., Ribas, C.C., Norgaard, R.B., Filizola, N., Ansar, A., Flyvbjerg, B. and Stevaux, J.C. (2017), 'Damming the rivers of the Amazon basin', *Nature* 546: 563–9 <https://www.nature.com/articles/nature22333>

Locatelli, P. (2015) 'Derrubar árvores para erguer hidrelétricas', *Repórter Brasil* [website] <http://reporterbrasil.org.br/2015/11/derrubar-arvores-para-erguer-hidreletricas>

Pierre-Louis, K. (2017) 'Dams on the Amazon river could have widespread, devastating impacts – and we keep building more of them', *Popular Science* [online] <https://www.popsci.com/environmental-damage-amazon-river-dams>

Repórter Brasil (2015) 'Respostas de Teles Pires', *Repórter Brasil* [online] <http://reporterbrasil.org.br/2015/11/respostas-de-teles-pires/>

UNFCCC (no date), 'Kyoto Protocol' *United Nations Framework Convention on Climate Change* [online] <https://unfccc.int/kyoto_protocol/items/2830.php>

UNFCCC (no date) 'United Nations, Project 9301: Teles Pires Hydropower Plant Project Activity' *United Nations Framework Convention on Climate Change* [website] <https://cdm.unfccc.int/Projects/DB/PJR%20CDM1356623851.07/view>

CHAPTER 5
The story of Sinop

Sinop today, with a population of 125,000, is a bustling town that services the region's wealthy soya farmers. Yet it is only 45 years old, set up by private land settlement businessmen attracted to the region by financial incentives from the military government. Before then, the region was inhabited by indigenous groups, particularly the Kayabi, many of whom fiercely resisted the occupation of their lands. Almost all the settlers, seeing themselves as pioneers, know nothing of this earlier history.

Visitors to the community of Sinop are greeted by a sign proclaiming: 'Sinop, capital of the North'. It's no empty boast: the well-planned city of 125,000, with its broad avenues and green spaces, dominates the local economy and is fast becoming the de facto capital of the northern part of the state of Mato Grosso. Sinop's citizens say the town's founders modelled it on Maringá, a garden city in Paraná state (originally designed by the British). Sinop today boasts numerous upmarket shops selling mobile phones, computers, and fashionable clothes. Car showrooms shine with expensive new vehicles, particularly pick-ups, able to handle the rough dirt roads that lead to the surrounding soya plantations and other farms. The stores – some flanked by Greek columns almost as large as the ones at the Parthenon, and even a replica of the Statue of Liberty – are not coy in broadcasting their message: we have great ambition and a lot of money to go with it.

What is not so clear – indeed, very surprising on a first visit – is that Sinop is only four decades old. A frontier town carved out in the north of Mato Grosso state, it is located in the Cerrado, a vast tropical savannah. While it forms part of the broad Amazon basin, called Amazônia Legal by the Brazilian authorities, it is not part of the Amazon biome, as the tropical forest is known. Sinop has a fascinating history that many young *sinopenses* know little about. The town's story is emblematic of the Amazon, where the region's natural riches are being incrementally culled year by year, decade by decade, and where the forest and indigenous people give way slowly to highways, dams, logging and mining operations, industrial agriculture, and small settlements that grow into cities.

From forest to boom town

In the first decades of the 20th century, indigenous people – particularly the Kayabi – inhabited the region where Sinop now stands. The Kayabi had long been considered wild and indomitable, as they had vigorously resisted the occupation of their land by rubber tappers, who, from the late 19th century, had been advancing north along the Paranatinga, as the upper Teles Pires was then known (ISA, n.d.). However, indigenous resistance was gradually worn down and some of the Indians were persuaded to work for the rubber companies. By then, the state government of Mato Grosso was beginning to divide a large part of the region into plots of land for non-indigenous settlers. The takeover of the region was under way.

It was at this time that the Villas Boas brothers encountered the Kayabi. These three brothers, who devoted their lives to the Indians, had become famous for getting the whole of the upper Xingu river turned into a legally protected area, the first huge indigenous area in South America. The brothers offered to resettle the Kayabi in the Xingu Indigenous Park, arguing that the alternative was detribalisation and marginalisation. Most of the Kayabi reluctantly agreed, though many still regret leaving their traditional land, particularly as the terrain and vegetation in the park are very different from those they were used to. Today, some of those who decided to stay share an indigenous reserve beside the Teles Pires river with the Munduruku and the Apiaká. Early Sinop settlers, who knew very little about the earlier indigenous occupation, told us that they recalled unearthing clay pots and indigenous axe heads when first clearing their land in the 1970s, but said that they encountered Indians only occasionally, as they passed through.

Under the Brazilian military government – which was obsessed with national security and fearful of a foreign takeover of the Amazon basin – the trickle of non-indigenous families to Mato Grosso state became a torrent. The nation's top generals adopted the slogan '*ocupar para não entregar*' ('occupy so as not to surrender') and took measures to ensure that the Amazon basin was populated with 'true Brazilians', their way of saying 'non-indigenous'. The generals had taken seriously a 1960s assessment by the New York-based Hudson Institute proposing that much of the Amazon basin be flooded to make mineral wealth accessible, a suggestion that, not surprisingly, the generals believed infringed Brazil's national sovereignty.

The military government provided tax incentives to encourage big companies (including, somewhat paradoxically, multinationals such as Volkswagen and Mercedes Benz) to cut down the rainforest and establish cattle ranches. They also funded the gigantic Transamazon Highway, which crossed the Amazon basin from east to west, and ordered the recently formed National Institute of Colonisation and Agrarian Reform (INCRA, Instituto Nacional de Colonização e Reforma Agrária) to settle landless families (brought in from the impoverished north-east of the country) along the road. The government also invited businessmen from Brazil's south, men with experience running private land settlement schemes, to set up similar operations in Mato Grosso. Vast swathes of forest gained 'owners': Zé Paraná in Juara, Ariosto da Riva in Alta Floresta, and Ênio Pipino in Sinop. All that stood in the way of these entrepreneurs, and a relentless wave of settlement and development, was the exuberant forest, the indigenous communities, and traditional populations – seen by the new landowners as mere obstacles to be overcome.

The Amazon's Wild West

Many of the large projects initiated by the government and by business failed to take root. The most successful were the private land settlements driven forward by the newly arrived big landowners. To encourage these businessmen, the military turned a blind eye to their crimes, which ranged from the violent eviction of peasants and Indians to large-scale land theft. Ênio Pipino was afforded exceptionally good treatment. Born into a family of Italian immigrants in 1917, he grew up in the state of São Paulo. In 1948, he set up the Northwestern Paraná Real Estate Society (Sociedade Imobiliaria Noroeste do Paraná), known as Sinop Terras. He bought large tracts of land very cheaply in the state of Paraná, then divided up the areas into plots, selling them to settlers at a considerable profit. Silvestre Duarte, who has studied the colonisation of Paraná, says it was a violent epoch: 'Paraná was like the American Wild West in the 19th century, when all conflicts were resolved by the bullet'. The level of violence used to drive out Indians and peasant families was so intense that it even drew a response in the Brazilian press and from the National Congress.

Pipino himself developed a reputation for ruthlessness, as he carved out an empire in northern Paraná. According to Duarte, 'From the middle of the 1940s to the beginning of the 1960s, Sinop's band

Photo 5.1 Sinop in 1973.
Photo by EduMarcelRibeiro/Creative Commons Attribution-ShareAlike 4.0 International license

of gunmen were very active in the region. Under the command of Marins Belo and other famous gunmen, they evicted entire families of squatters and assassinated many people, throwing their bodies into the Piquiri river. Indeed, this became the hallmark of Sinop's hired guns'. By all accounts, Pipino became very rich.

The businessman then began planning how he could replicate his Paraná settlements on a bigger scale in Mato Grosso. The Sinop archivist, Luiz Erardi, told us that in 1970 Pipino and his wife, Lélia Maria de Araújo Vieira, began paying visits to the region. Encouraged by what they saw, Pipino bought some land from an absentee landowner and opened up rough roads to make it accessible. He carved out plots to sell and opened real estate offices in the state of Paraná, promoting his Mato Grosso land with newspaper advertisements and radio jingles. Relying on military support, Pipino took over more land, much of it lacking titles. It seems likely that he used methods similar to those he employed in Paraná in the even more lawless Mato Grosso. Erardi confirmed that Pipino had evicted peasant families, though he did not comment on the methods used. Although ruthless, Pipino could also be charming, according to Sinop residents who remember him, and he had a salesman's knack for putting people's minds at rest. One early settler, Geraldino Dal'Mazo, told us that people felt reassured when Pipino guaranteed them a plot with a legal land title. His right to issue such titles was, at best, dubious.

An influx of eco-refugees, a hard life

In 1972, the first settlers made the arduous seven-day trip from Paraná to Mato Grosso. Many sent dispirited reports back home, saying how difficult life was in the Amazon. Then came 1975 and a severe frost in Paraná that wiped out the coffee harvest. 'That frost ended forever coffee cultivation in Paraná', said Luiz Erardi. 'Many families began to think seriously about moving north. Big landowners were arriving with tempting offers: "I'll give you so much for your land!" Many say that with [the sale of] their tiny plot in Paraná they bought a sizeable farm in Mato Grosso'.

Everyday life on the Amazon agricultural frontier remained arduous. There was no proper health service and no schools. The forest soils were infertile. There was no technical support and settlers found that the farming skills they had acquired in the south didn't transplant to the Amazon. Relieved that there were no frosts, some planted coffee, only to see it fail for other reasons, often the excessive rain. Many gave up. 'They came penniless and went back doubly so', Erardi said. Broke, they often had to find a neighbour with a lorry and persuade him to transport them back to their home state, paying him with the only thing they had left – their land. Almost worthless then, those plots have since risen hugely in value, and today the children and grand-children of the lorry drivers have grown rich on the appreciation.

Luiz Erardi and his wife arrived in 1982 to work as teachers and found life very hard. Their diesel generator broke often; they didn't have hot water; there was no stove in the kitchen. 'Two months after we arrived, I woke one morning, opened the wooden shutters in our shack, and saw that everything around us was flooded. I went to make coffee and the sugar had turned to syrup. I said to myself: "This is a land for frogs, not people"'. The floods were the final straw. 'I told my wife we had to leave that morning. I couldn't stand it any more. But she refused. She said she hadn't wanted to come but now she was here she wasn't giving up. She stamped her foot and said: "I'm not leaving". And we didn't. Thank goodness'. Geraldino Dal'Mazo, who arrived in 1985 (and died of cancer in December 2016, shortly after we spoke to him), had a similar experience. After a few weeks in Sinop, he had had enough: 'One day, I decided we were leaving, but my wife, who's a real fighter, was having none of it: "We're not going", she said. "Even if I have to work as a washerwoman and you have to till the land for others, we're staying. I didn't want to come. We lived in comfort in Paraná. But now we're here, we're not going"'. They too stayed, and never looked back.

A presidential saviour

After a few difficult years, Sinop prospered, along with Pipino, who was always after more land, though the legality of his claims was often dubious. At one point, he is known to have laid claim to at least 645,000 hectares. In a letter dated 25 March 1979, found in the INCRA archive in Brasília, Pipino courteously requests Paulo Yakota, the then president of INCRA, to give him the title to a two-million hectare plot called Gleba Celeste. The request seems to have been partially granted: Gleba Celeste was registered in Pipino's name, though covering just a third of the requested size. As in Paraná, Pipino founded many new towns for his settlers, giving them all women's names – Vera, Cláudia, and Santa Carmem.

Pipino also used his influence to garner government favour, especially with General Figueiredo, who ruled Brazil from 1979 to 1985. 'Who got this region to prosper was President João Baptista Figueiredo', declared Geraldino Dal'Mazo. 'He came in 1979 and saw our suffering'. The visiting president made a commitment to paving the recently built BR-163 highway, proclaiming he would bring asphalt. Figueiredo contracted five construction companies from Cuiabá and two years later he came and personally opened the road. 'We didn't have a television signal or telephones ... And he sorted that out on the plane. We had them in four months. And with that, Sinop took off ... President Figueiredo was marvellous. We made him an honorary citizen of Sinop', remembered Dal'Mazo.

Still, not everyone thrived. Locals say that it was the pig-headed who stayed and reaped the rewards, but to become a millionaire on the frontier generally required more than stubbornness. University teacher Maria Ivonete de Souza related how her father, an impoverished rural labourer, was given a plot at one of the land settlements. 'It was difficult for settlers who arrived without capital', she said. 'Forty years later my father is just as poor as when he arrived. He's always had to work on someone else's land to make ends meet'.

Photo 5.2 Sinop as it is today.
Photo by Sinop Municipal Government website

Both Geraldino Dal'Mazo and Luiz Erardi were happy they stayed. Luiz Erardi, who got a series of good municipal government jobs, is proud to have a granddaughter who has trained as a medical doctor. Geraldino Dal'Mazo made a lot of money in the early years, opening up petrol stations, and became mayor during the military government. Then he lost his fortune when the Brazilian economy went through a difficult period in the early 1980s. His children, however, almost all of whom stayed in the region, have done very well.

Sinop's shining success

Sinop has carved out a key role for itself as service provider to a vast area, stretching north from Cuiabá, in the south of Mato Grosso, all the way to Pará. People send their children to Sinop's colleges and university, and value its hospitals. The region's farmers, after experimenting and failing with various crops (including cassava for a large alcohol distillery, which went bankrupt), eventually hit the jackpot. Geraldino Dal'Mazo's brother was the first to try growing soya, which until the 1980s was little known in Brazil. 'He planted 1,500 hectares in 1987 and had a marvellous harvest', recalled Dal'Mazo. Now most farmers cultivate soya, complementing that crop with corn and cotton in the off-season.

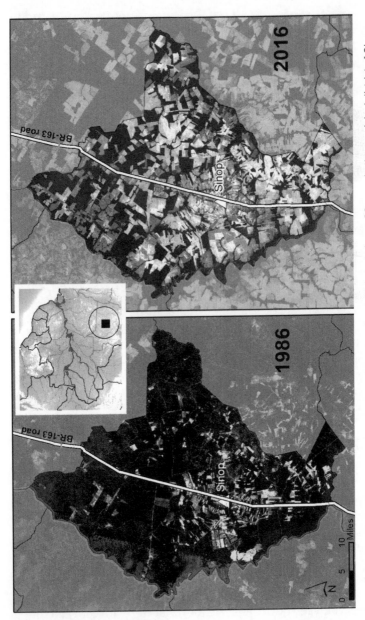

Map 5.1 Comparison of forest cover (dark areas) and clear-cut forest (light areas) over 30 years in the municipal district of Sinop. Map by Mauricio Torres

Today, Sinop belongs to modern Brazil, and those who paid a heavy price for the city's success – indigenous nations, landless peasant families, and undercapitalised settlers – are largely invisible. The cost to the ecosystem is more obvious: the blanket of vegetation that covered the Sinop region until the 1970s is largely gone, replaced by heavily fertilised and hyper-managed soya plantations. Where once forest stood untouched, today only a third of the area of the Sinop municipal district is still covered with trees. Depending on your point of view, Sinop is a wild territory tamed, or a great wilderness and indigenous homeland devastated by modern development.

Travelling further north from Sinop along the BR-163 highway is like travelling into Sinop's past. When crossing the border into Pará state, one reaches the current frontier, where the battle over the land is still being waged, and where fragile indigenous cultures and ecosystems are being consumed in smouldering violence on a daily basis. But before we moved north we decided to investigate more fully the arrival of soya into the state of Mato Grosso. And this is the issue we cover in the next two chapters.

Reference

ISA (no date) 'Povos Indígenas no Brasil', *Instituto Socioambiental (ISA)* <https://pib.socioambiental.org/en/povo/kawaiwete/273> [Last accessed July 2018]

CHAPTER 6
Soya invades the Cerrado

In less than 50 years, agribusiness, predominantly large-scale soya farming, has destroyed almost half of the original vegetation of the Cerrado, Brazil's vast tropical savannah, along with much of its biodiversity. Now, with agribusiness lobbyists pressing hard for an ambitious transport infrastructure of highways, railways, and industrial waterways to facilitate the export of commodities, the Amazon forest too is under growing threat.

The vast tropical savannah known as the Cerrado covers over two million square kilometres, an area four times as large as Spain. It lies to the south and the east of the Amazon biome in Brazil's centre-west region and covers large areas of various states, including Mato Grosso. Co-author Sue Branford first came to the Cerrado in 1974, when she travelled in a military lorry from Cuiabá, the capital of Mato Grosso, to Sinop, which was at the time a tiny frontier settlement of no more than 15 shacks. The military government in power at the time was opening up the region, and the lorry was bringing in supplies. For four days, they bumped up and down on a deeply potholed track, forced several times to dig themselves out of ruts. They saw few people, just a few resilient peasant families practising slash-and-burn agriculture. All around was dense vegetation, with occasional natural clearings. People said there were Indians living in the forest, but they didn't see any.

In October 2016, 36 years later, Sue made the same journey, this time travelling in an air-conditioned bus. The region was completely transformed. The bus travelled smoothly along a paved highway. There were scarcely any trees, just endless soya plantations, with occasional silos emblazoned with the logos of the grain companies that now dominate the region: Bunge, Archer Daniels Midland (ADM), Cargill, and the sole Brazilian company – Amaggi. It was a powerful demonstration of how soya has taken over the region.

Despised for centuries as worthless for farming, the Cerrado has become the pride of Brazilian agribusiness, achieving one of the world's highest levels of productivity. In the process of incorporating this savannah into the country's farming lands, almost half of its

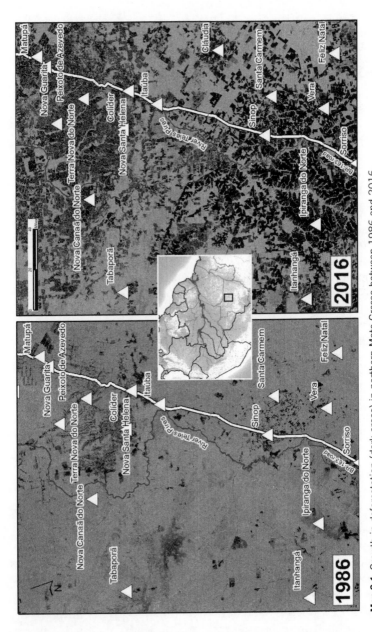

Map 6.1 Growth in deforestation (dark areas) in northern Mato Grosso between 1986 and 2016. Map by Maurício Torres

biodiversity was destroyed. 'It suffered an extremely fast process of deforestation, unprecedented in the country', said Laerte Ferreira, from the Geoprocessing Laboratory at the Federal University of Goiás (Ciscati, 2017).

Thanks in large part to the Cerrado's development, Brazil has become a leading exporter of agricultural products. By 2013, the country's agricultural and food exports amounted to US$89.5 bn, more than six times the US$14.3 bn reached in the year 2000. Brazil had by then become the world's largest exporter of the soya complex (beans, meal, and oil), overtaking the United States (Ray and Schaffer, 2017). Largely because demand from Asia, particularly from China, is expected to continue growing, Brazil is poised to become the world's largest exporter of agricultural and food products by 2024, according to the OECD–FAO Agricultural Outlook 2015–2024 (FAO, 2015). This is largely because Brazil is seen as having a 'large available land base to produce soybeans' which is something that its main competitors – the USA and Argentina – lack.

But it is only agribusiness that sees this land as 'available'. Most other people – environmentalists, natural scientists, sociologists, the affected populations, and many others – are fiercely opposed to the further environmental destruction that would stem from increased soya cultivation. The Cerrado, which used to possess an extraordinary biodiversity, with 13,000 species of plants, 850 species of birds, and 250 species of mammals, has already paid a very heavy price; many of its drought- and fire-resistant plants, endemic bird species, and large mammals, including giant anteaters, giant armadillos, and jaguars, are now threatened with extinction (Mansur, 2017). Thousands of families have also been thrown off their plots of land, with an alarming increase in violence as they fought back. Since many key rivers have their headwaters in the Cerrado, scientists are also concerned that further destruction will have significant impacts on vast areas downstream.

The drive to find more land for export crops is moving into the Amazon forest. As will be discussed later, this brings a huge risk to both Brazil and the world, as the forest is very close to the tipping point at which it will start to die, with a calamitous impact on the global climate. The region is also home to countless traditional communities of riverine families, rubber tappers, Brazil nut collectors, and peasant farmers, as well as to many remarkable indigenous peoples. As all travellers in the Amazon know, there is no such thing as empty land.

Each tract of forest is used in some way, even if it isn't inhabited. For instance, for some local people the special vines, used in the building of their traditional wooden houses, constructed without nails, can be found only in very specific areas.

Whereas large-scale farmers in the south of the Cerrado have been happy to take their bounty to market through the ports of Santos in São Paulo state and Paranaguá in Paraná state in southern Brazil, those in northern Mato Grosso have been increasingly alarmed at the cost, as their harvest has followed a circuitous 1,500-mile route, being trucked over hot, pothole-ridden roads to the Atlantic Ocean ports, only to be transported north again to markets in Europe and Asia. Ever since they first moved into the north of Mato Grosso in the late 1990s, agribusiness has dreamed of reducing these high transport costs by finding a way of creating new export corridors through the state of Pará. They have thought up three ways of achieving this: the paving of the BR-163 highway (which links the cities of Cuiabá and Santarém); the building of a new railroad (officially called EF-170 but universally known by its nickname *Ferrogrão*, or Grainrail), which would run parallel to the road; and, most ambitiously of all, the building of a Teles Pires–Tapajós industrial waterway, a mega-project requiring the dredging of the rivers, the dynamiting of rapids, and dozens of huge dams, reservoirs, locks, canals, and river ports.

Carlos Fávaro, president of Aprosoja, Brazil's largest soya bean co-operative, and vice-president of Mato Grosso state, has long been an enthusiastic supporter of the third option, which many environmentalists believe would be the most damaging of all. Speaking glowingly of the Tapajós as 'Brazil's Mississippi' and as a 'gift from God', he declares that Brazil has been bequeathed by nature with a river that flows north which, once tamed, will allow for the transport of crops by barge and container ship from the country's largest agricultural region in Central Brazil to the Amazon river and on to ports on the Atlantic Ocean – making the export routes to China, other Asian nations, and European markets dramatically shorter and cheaper (Lovatelli and Fávaro, 2012).

Some people credit soya production with bringing modernity and development to Mato Grosso. Aprosoja speaks of 'the positive socioeconomic impact of soya farming'. It claims that for each person directly engaged in soya farming, another 11 jobs are created, 'taking into account all the employment produced along the whole productive chain' (Aprosoja, n.d.). In 2012, Blairo Maggi, senator for

Mato Grosso state at the time, told the *Folha de S. Paulo* newspaper: 'If it weren't for soya, Mato Grosso would still be backward ... Today the soya farmer gets a 30 per cent return on the capital he invests' (Kachani, 2017).

But for others, the 40-year soya expansion serves as just one more example in a long historical process in which savannah and rainforest are being cut down and rural indigenous and traditional populations disenfranchised, to be replaced by agribusiness monocultures owned by a very few, who take the lion's share of profit. The sociologist José de Souza Martins, whose writings have become essential reading for Amazon scholars, showed that, while the military government in the 1970s spoke a great deal about attracting landless farmers to the Amazon (under the slogan 'the land without people for the people without land'), powerful economic groups were the main beneficiaries of the money it poured into the region (Martins, 1985). This meant that, far from 'occupying the empty land', the generals facilitated the creation of large cattle ranches that drove out many more people – including the 'invisible' indigenous communities, rubber tappers, and fisher folk – than they brought into the region.

Cândido Neto da Cunha, an agronomist employed by INCRA, believes that what is happening with soya now is, to a large extent, just a continuation of the military programmes. 'Though development has replaced national security as the ideological driving force, the state is, today, through its support for agribusiness, creating the same negative social consequences – rural exodus, deforestation, and precarious labour conditions', he said.

China's hunger for soya

The unchecked, ever-rising global demand for soya creates a bleak outlook for the Amazon rainforest and its indigenous and traditional communities. The driving force behind the advance of soya in Brazilian territory is Chinese demand and policy. Up to 1995, China was self-sufficient in soya (Brown, 2013). But that year the country's human population outpaced food crop production, and the government decided to prioritise crops. It upped the in-country production of human foods – wheat, rice, and corn – and reduced soya production, most of which is fed to animals. The motive was simple: the people and government still remembered the Great Famine of 1959–61, when millions starved to death, and so were fearful of relying on imported food. The impact of the policy shift was immediate: by 2011, China was importing 56 million tons of soya. Since then, demand has continued growing: China is expected to import 102 million tons in 2017 and probably 180 million tons by 2024 – more than the combined current output of the world's three largest growers (the USA, Brazil, and Argentina) (Maverick, 2014).

Where will this production come from? It is unlikely that the USA can increase its production, and analysts have been saying since 2010 that the area under soya cultivation in Argentina cannot grow significantly (Brown, 2013). That leaves Brazil to fill the gap. Until recently, Brazil significantly increased its soya output primarily through rises in per-acre productivity, but there seems little room for further improvements here: since 2000, Brazil's soya productivity has stabilized at about three tons per hectare (Lucidarium Blog, 2012). The only option, then, for meeting China's demands, argued Lester Brown, president of the Earth Policy Institute at the time, is to push the agricultural frontier deeper into the Amazon forest. That's a goal also totally in keeping with the plans of the politically powerful *Bancada Ruralista*, which dominates the current Brazilian government.

The anthropologist Rinaldo Arruda is deeply alarmed by the prospects of a 21st century soya invasion deep into Amazonia's heart. He envisages 'cities swelled with people, without sanitation, very violent places, with internal conflicts and degraded environments. A shanty town Amazonia.... This notion that our society has, at least from the 19th century, of becoming more and more civilised is profoundly mistaken. It doesn't exist. It's a fiction'.

There is much talk about the prosperity that agribusiness has brought to Mato Grosso state (Kipper et al., 2015), but, according to Andreia Fanzeres, co-ordinator of the indigenous rights programme at OPAN, the traditional communities, which had inhabited the region for centuries, were not consulted, nor have they benefited from the rise of soya: 'The indigenous communities and the family farmers – rural communities in general – were always outside the decision-making process as to what type of development they would have'.

While this broader picture describes the northward thrust of agribusiness, marching like a single army, there are other ways in which soya can infiltrate a region by circuitous, unexpected routes, rarely reported in the press. It is to these we turn in the next chapter.

References

All web references were checked and still available in June/July 2018 unless otherwise stated.

Aprosoja Brasil (no date) 'Uso da Soja', *Aprosoja Brasil* [website] <http://aprosojabrasil.com.br/2014/sobre-a-soja/uso-da-soja/>

Brown, L. (2013) 'How China's rising soybean consumption is reshaping western agriculture', *Treehugger* [website] <https://www.treehugger.com/sustainable-agriculture/chinas-rising-soybean-consumption-reshaping-western-agriculture.html>

Ciscati, R. (2017) 'Como a destruição do Cerrado pode fazer faltar água no Brasil inteiro', Época 27 March 2017 <https://epoca.globo.com/ciencia-e-meio-ambiente/blog-do-planeta/noticia/2017/03/como-destruicao-do-cerrado-pode-fazer-faltar-agua-no-brasil-inteiro.html>

FAO (2015) 'OECD-FAO Agricultural Outlook 2015' *OECD and FAO* [Report] <http://www.oecd-ilibrary.org/agriculture-and-food/oecd-fao-agricultural-outlook-2015_agr_outlook-2015-en;jsessionid=x2h7cfymubhn.x-oecd-live-02>

Kachani, M. (2017) 'Contradições marcam o progresso de Mato Grosso', *Folha de S. Paulo* <http://www1.folha.uol.com.br/fsp/mercado/45223-contradicoes-marcam-o-progresso-de-mato-grosso.shtml>

Kipper, A., Paludo, S. and Cammarota, F. (2015) 'Agronegócio para o desenvolvimento do estado do Mato Grosso', *VIII Congresso CONSAD de Gestão Pública* 26–28 May 2015, [Report] <http://www.escoladegestao.pr.gov.br/arquivos/File/2015/VIII_Consad/041.pdf>

Lovatelli, C. and Fávaro C. (2012) 'As eclusas na ampliação do modal hidroviário', *O Estado de S. Paulo* <https://opiniao.estadao.com.br/noticias/geral,as-eclusas-na-ampliacao-do-modal-hidroviario-imp-,893783>

Lucidarium Blog (2012) 'Vinte anos de cultivo da soja em Mato Grosso', *Cicero* [blog] <https://lucidarium.com.br/2012/09/22/vinte-anos-de-cultivo-da-soja-em-mato-grosso/>

Mansur, A. (2017) 'Desmatamento do Cerrado', *Época* 20 May 2017 <https://epoca.globo.com/tudo-sobre/noticia/2017/05/desmatamento-do-cerrado.html>

Martins, J.S. (1985) *A militarização da reforma agrária*, Petrópolis.

Maverick, T. (2014) 'China's hunger for soy to exceed global supply', *Wall Street Daily* [Article] <https://www.wallstreetdaily.com/2014/11/11/china-soybean-futures/>

Ray, D.E. and Schaffer, H.D. (2017) 'Brazil seeks to become the world's largest agricultural exporter', *Momagri* [Website] <http://www.momagri.org/UK/focus-on-issues/Brazil-seeks-to-become-the-world-s-largest-agricultural-exporter_1634.html>

CHAPTER 7

The threat to the Amazon

Soya farmers are using different wheezes to facilitate their penetration of the Amazon forest. These range from bribery, to gain access to agrarian reform settlements, to largely unnoticed changes in legislation that make it much easier for them to take over land legally.

In its march north, soya appears in some surprising places. One of these is at the Wesley Manoel dos Santos agrarian reform settlement, created by INCRA in 1977. Located 70 kilometres (43 miles) north-west of Sinop, this settlement exemplifies the serious challenges faced by Brazil's small family farms, and how soya farmers can take advantage of these difficulties to worm themselves in to areas from which they are banned.

The land was originally bought up by the Brazilian subsidiary of the German company Mercedes Benz, at the end of the 1960s. According to research by Odimar João Peripolli, a lecturer at Mato Grosso State University, the company set up 10 separate subsidiary companies to circumvent legal limits on land ownership. Each subsidiary bought '40,000, 50,000, or even 60,000 hectares, so that in the end it [Mercedes Benz] had acquired about 500,000 hectares (1.2 million acres). The whole large estate became known as *Gleba Mercedes* (the Mercedes Holding)' (Peripolli, 2008). The company was able to use its clout as a large-scale landowner to gain hefty federal benefits, mostly tax rebates from the Amazonia Development Superintendency (SUDAM, Superintendência do Desenvolvimento da Amazônia). This money was supposed to be used to make the land productive, but wasn't, according to testimonies gathered by Peripolli. The company's vast holdings were 'never, effectively, occupied by the company', he said. Mercedes eventually sold *Gleba Mercedes* to a São Paulo company, which in turn sold it to INCRA, which created an agrarian reform settlement with plots for 507 families.

It's not easy for a small-scale farm settlement to compete economically in a remote region where the government is actively promoting large-scale agribusiness. Lacking sufficient technical assistance from the government, the settlement's 500-plus families tried several survival strategies. In the beginning, they reared dairy cattle and sold milk and cheese in Sinop. Though this was the nearest market, it still took three hours to transport dairy products there – and that was when it wasn't raining.

The venture went well at first, but then ran into government obstacles. Settler Jair Marcelo da Silva, known as Capixava, relates how the small-scale dairy farmers were very careful with hygiene, because it was their principle to sell only products that they themselves consumed. However, their common-sense approach didn't satisfy the authorities. 'The food safety bodies don't think like ordinary people, they think very differently', says Capixava. The authorities made exacting regulatory demands on the small-scale farmers, including unrealistically tough hygiene requirements, and, when they couldn't satisfy those demands, the settlers were banned from selling their produce in Sinop. It was the end of their dreams. 'I had six cows, from which I took on average 90 litres of milk a day', explains Capixava. 'What was I supposed to do with this milk [if the federal authorities wouldn't let me sell it]? What do you think? We gave it to the pigs! Just imagine that!'

The settlers tried rearing pigs and chickens, but once again they fell foul of food safety regulators. Lacking any other income, some settlers trained to operate the sophisticated machines used by the large-scale farmers who had the money to comply with government health and safety rules. Others worked as day labourers. Women found jobs as maids in Sinop, leaving their husbands to look after the children. In time, attempts to use their land to earn a living were largely abandoned.

Shortly afterwards, the vacant land of the agrarian reform settlement caught the eye of big soya farmers, and the impoverished settlers began renting their plots for next to nothing to the soya producers. This might seem a foolish deal but, in exchange, the large-scale soya farmers 'tamed the land'. This expression, frequently heard in the region, describes the elimination of native vegetation, the digging out of tree roots, and the use of chemicals to reduce soil acidity – an expensive land-preparation process that takes at least three years. So a poor settler got his cropland cleared of forest, something he couldn't afford to do for himself, and, in a world where land stripped of native vegetation is worth much more than standing forest, the settler ended up with a far more valuable asset. Though, of course, he didn't end up with the soya crop; those profits went to the large-scale farmers.

Soya also arrived in the agrarian reform settlement by a more circuitous, less legal route. During our visit in November 2016, we noticed an enormous soya plantation, much too big to belong to a single settler. Capixava explained how it got there. By law, all settlers must keep a portion of their land as forest, and INCRA had decreed that it made more sense, from an ecological point of view, to bring all these forest lots together in a single collective reserve. Capixava said that, in the early days, the forest in their collective reserve was 'so dense that fire never penetrated it'.

But what fire couldn't achieve the big soya farmers did. Caixava said that the soya farmers used the *correntão* – an enormous chain, 100 metres long, suspended between two huge tractors, which, when pulled along, uproots all the forest in its path. The illegally-cleared 3,500-hectare area is now completely covered in soya. Nobody knows for sure how this obviously illegal action happened, but many settlers say that a corrupt INCRA employee ceded the forest reserve to the soya farmers and then bought himself a mansion in Barra do Garças, a town in the south of the state, with his unlawful profits.

Gleba Mercedes is not an isolated case. The criminal advance of agribusiness into agrarian reform settlements has happened elsewhere. For instance, the Terra Prometida Operation, launched by the federal police in November 2004, led to the arrest of more than 20 people in the Tapuráh–Itanhangá settlement to the west of Sinop (Werneck, 2014). According to police, the soya farmers had taken over more than 1,000 of the 1,149 settler plots, and had created a giant soya plantation. Among those arrested were Odair and Milton Geller, brothers of then Agriculture Minister Neri Geller, who is currently the ministry's secretary for agrarian policy.

The geographer Antônio Loris believes that this kind of illegal action has become accepted and sees little chance of reform, because agribusiness is 'intrinsically corrupt'. He asserts that 'there is a very evident and immediate form of corruption (as in the way INCRA is controlled by landowners and land thieves), but there is also a long-term form of corruption, expressed in the violent appropriation of land, aggressiveness against squatters and Indians, and social and environmental destruction'.

Christmas comes early for the land thieves

Recent changes in the law may mean that these kinds of practices become much more widespread. Under the Brazilian Constitution, a settler in an agrarian reform settlement cannot sell his land title for 10 years. This means, for example, that it was illegal for agribusiness to buy the plots in the Tapuráh–Itanhangá settlement because, although the settlement was created in 1997, almost all the beneficiaries had held their plot titles for less than 10 years.

In December 2016, however, the Temer administration issued a presidential decree (MP 759), which altered the way land titles are issued. The decree largely dealt with the chaotic housing situation in the poor districts that have sprung up around most of Brazil's large cities. Because MP 759 will make it easier for some people to register their land ownership, it was welcomed by some lawyers, with one calling it President Temer's 'Christmas present'. Bruno Araújo, Brazil's Minister for Cities, said that by allowing poor urban dwellers to get titles for their land more quickly, the decree will put 'millions of assets into the economy' (Pereira, 2016).

But, unnoticed by most observers, the decree also altered how the 10-year term is counted in agrarian reform settlements. Under the old system, the term began only once the structure of the settlement was in place and the settler had received his or her land title; now the counting starts when the family receives formal notification that it has been given a plot. It may seem an unimportant bureaucratic adjustment, but agronomist Cândido Neto da Cunha believes it to be highly significant: 'MP 759 is clearly intended to legalise the illegal occupation of agrarian reform land and to put more of the plots on the market', he says. Cunha says the settlements don't receive the support they need from the federal government, and this weakens the settlers economically. 'They become more vulnerable to pressure to sell their land in areas where agribusiness is expanding', he explains.

Together with soya's penetration of the region, the big grain companies and the Brazilian government are investing a great deal in the construction of export corridors for the soya and the maize. It is to this that we turn in the next chapter.

References

All web references were checked and still available in June/July 2018 unless otherwise stated.

Pereira, J. (2016) 'Governo publica medida provisória com regras para regularização fundiária urbana e rural', *Congressoemfoco* [website] <http://congressoemfoco.uol.com.br/noticias/governo-publica-mp-com-regras-para-regularizacao-fundiaria-urbana-e-rural/>

Peripolli, O.J. (2008) *Expansão do capitalismo na Amazônia norte mato-grossense: a mercantilização da terra e da escola*, Ph.D. thesis, Universidade Federal do Rio Grande do Sul

Werneck, K. (2014) 'MT: ilegais do agronegócio grilam terras públicas de R$ 1 bi', *Terra* 27 November 2014 <https://www.terra.com.br/noticias/brasil/policia/mt-ilegais-do-agronegocio-grilam-terras-publicas-de-r-1-bi,081ad9f8523f9410VgnVCM10000098cceb0aRCRD.html>

CHAPTER 8
The soya transport corridor

With the rapid expansion of soya production in Mato Grosso state and into the Amazon basin, agribusiness and international grain companies became increasingly aware at the beginning of this century of the need for an effective transport corridor to the north, to take crops to the Amazon river for export. Despite bickering between themselves, a huge new transport infrastructure has been created, with support from the government.

Santarém is one of the Amazon's oldest towns, inhabited for centuries by a thriving and populous Amerindian community, but officially founded in 1661 by the Jesuits. It lies close to the famous meeting of the waters, where for several miles the greenish waters of the Tapajós river run parallel with, then flow into, the red-brown stream of the Amazon. The town long served as a departure point for adventurers and traders heading for the Amazonian wild. Until recently, it exuded an attractive, old-fashioned beauty with its dilapidated colonial buildings, a riverside market where locals hawked freshly caught fish, herbal remedies, and indigenous handicrafts, and a bustling river port where small fishing boats and canoes mixed with elegant three-storey riverboats packed with passengers lounging in hammocks, ready for the voyage ahead. The river beckoned, then. After all, it was the main way to get anywhere.

But in 2003, all this began to change with the construction of a large grain terminal built by Cargill, the largest private company in the US. Though the terminal stayed unused for many years, trucks laden with soya and maize from Mato Grosso state gradually began to struggle along the rugged, rutted BR-163 highway, bringing noise and congestion as they cut through the town to reach it. Although Santarém itself was later to be somewhat marginalised as an Amazon transport hub, these events heralded a new future for the Tapajós basin. Agribusiness in Brazil's interior had at last found a cheaper way to move farm commodities north by road to the Tapajós and Amazon rivers, then on, in barges, to the Atlantic coast and to lucrative commodity markets abroad – sparking growth in Pará state that has been gaining force ever since.

Photo 8.1 Cargill's soya terminal in Santarém.
Photo by Walter Guimarães

Road routes for the soya trucks

It wasn't Cargill but the state-owned agricultural research company EMBRAPA (Empresa Brasileira de Pesquisa Agropecuária) that first brought agribusiness to Brazil's interior – first to the state of Mato Grosso and then further north to the state of Pará. EMBRAPA provided excellent technical services, helping to improve the soils, providing crop varieties adapted to the Cerrado, and supplying chemical fertilisers. Next came Monsanto, and later the other biotechnology companies, furnishing large-scale farmers with technological packages – all-in-one set-ups including genetically modified (GM) seed, fertiliser, and pesticide, along with a guarantee to purchase the crop.

With the expansion of agribusiness in Brazil's interior and its increasing dominance in the Brazilian economy, it became clear that Mato Grosso and Pará needed a much better transport infrastructure to deliver the goods, something seen to be obvious as early as 1994 by commodities analyst Jorge Baldo. During our Tapajós visit in November 2016, we met him, a self-taught man and a passionate nationalist, in the town of Sorriso, located along the BR-163 in Mato Grosso. Sitting at his desk, a military coat of arms on the wall behind, he told us that the farming sector in Sorriso, which was very small in the early 1990s, went through a serious crisis in 1994, just like agriculture all

Photo 8.2 A sign welcomes drivers to the city of Sorriso, Brazil's agribusiness capital.
Photo by Thaís Borges

Photo 8.3 Jorge Baldo.
Photo by Thaís Borges

over Brazil. The Bank of Brazil was prepared to roll over the farmers' debts to help them, recalled Baldo, but he realised that this aid by itself would not be enough: 'The producers needed inputs. And we didn't have a road! It took a week for anything to come from Cuiabá!'

Baldo began calling for heavy investments to make the southern portion of the BR-163 passable all year round – a project regarded as utopian as the road, though nominally asphalted, was little more than a series of mud ruts through the rainforest. 'Little by little, we won over one person and then another, created the pro-BR-163 Committee, and we started to make demands', he remembered. Slowly, the BR-163 was properly asphalted, with the paving moving north from Cuiabá, but it took until 2007 before Sorriso had a reliable transport link to the south. Finally, the town had the conditions it needed to become Brazil's agribusiness capital.

BR-163's asphalt allowed Mato Grosso's crops, as we have seen, to be exported south along potholed roads to Santos and Paranaguá on the Atlantic coast. There, the commodities were transferred to transatlantic vessels, in which they travelled back north for another 2,400 kilometres (1,400 miles) before going east to Europe or west through the Panama Canal to China. This lengthy trip was expensive and unreliable: docks in the southern ports were often so crowded that the trucks could wait up to 60 days to be unloaded (Freitas and Wilson, 2014).

Agribusiness became increasingly frustrated by the cost and delays of the southern route, realising that if the commodity-laden trucks could just roll north along the then unpaved northern section of BR-163, they could cut the trucking distance in half by unloading their cargo into ships at Santarém on the Amazon river. But, at the time, the highway north to Santarém was very precarious in summer and utterly impassable in the winter rainy season. Travelling along the BR-163 in 2004, taking almost three days to cover a mere 140 kilometres (85 miles), stuck in the ruts with hundreds of other lorries and cars, we had to choose between sweltering inside our vehicle or being devoured by mosquitoes outside. Two members of our group contracted malaria. It became clear to us that, as an export route, the unpaved northern part of BR-163 was unviable.

That's when Blairo Maggi came up with an interim solution. Maggi, who even then was a political force to be reckoned with in Mato Grosso, and who now serves as Brazil's agriculture minister, had the highly controversial MT-235 road built through the Utiariti indigenous reserve, creating a new transport link along which soya could travel north-west by lorry to the Madeira river and then north-east by barge to Santarém. This served the interests of the Maggi family well, as they had already invested heavily in soya, as well as some other farmers in the region too. But it was logistical nonsense for the farmers in the northern part of the state, whose beans were now driven along two sides of a triangle to get to market. Even so, the farmers said, it was better than taking the soya south.

Cargill was the first grain trader to bet on the exit to the north, building its terminal in 2003 on an archaeological site within Santarém. But, according to Cargill's Clythio Buggenhout, because the BR-163 was impassable, Cargill too was forced in the early days to use the indirect MT-235–Madeira river transport link opened up by Maggi (Amazônia Notícias e Informação, 2013). The MT-235 was not the only road Maggi built. Throughout our November 2016 journey, farmers told us about the logistical help the politician offered, particularly when he was Mato Grosso's state governor from 2003 to 2010. Dal'Mazo, former mayor of Sinop, told us: 'Blairo Maggi is a very intelligent person. He always helped the region ... He opened roads for his own products, but then he let everyone use them. So why would anyone complain?'

In 2003, President Lula's Workers' Party finally announced plans to pave the northern section of BR-163. In response, the multinational grain companies rushed to open terminals on the Tapajós river. Bunge was there first, constructing a transhipment terminal in the new port of Miritituba, opposite the town of Itaituba. At last, transport logistics for commodities were beginning to make sense. The road north was 1,000 kilometres (650 miles) shorter than the route south, and the new port meant that trucks could unload their cargo onto barges, which travelled down the lower Tapajós to the Amazon river, and then east to the ports of Barcarena, near Belém, and Santana, near Macapá, the capital of Amapá state.

Bunge then carried out a master stroke against competitor Cargill. It sold half the assets in its Miritituba–Barcarena complex to Amaggi, the Brazilian company belonging to Blairo Maggi's family, dramatically increasing Amaggi's stake in the export business – which is where the greatest profits are to be made. 'This new step strengthens our presence in the region and also contributes to the growth of a key logistics route', declared Amaggi CEO Waldemir Loto at the time (Oils & Fats International Magazine, 2016). But, in truth, while the deal benefited Amaggi, it was even better for Bunge, because Blairo

Maggi immediately put his political muscle, along with large sums of public money, behind the Miritituba–Barcarena river port complex. In 2004, the government (apparently pressured by Maggi) announced that the last 172 kilometres (107 miles) of the BR-163, taking it to Santarém, would not be paved. Cargill's Santarém terminal was now stranded at the end of a muddy road, and commodities traffic started flowing instead to Miritituba, where the asphalt ended. The governor of Pará, Simão Jatene, protested: 'The largest city in the lower Amazon cannot be excluded from the paving of the BR-163!' (Brasiliense, 2004). But excluded Santarém was, and Cargill was eventually forced to build its own terminal in Miritituba. 'Miritituba is an obvious road-and-river entrepôt, it's a meeting point', declared Cargill Director Clythio Buggenhout in 2013, 'it opens a range of logistic alternatives' (Amazônia Notícias e Informação, 2013).

Roadkill: local people and the rainforest

The preparation and construction of all this transport infrastructure has come at a price. The first victim was the rainforest. In the year following Lula's announcement of the paving of the northern part of BR-163, forest clearing exploded, particularly on either side of the road. 'Ten years later, the levels of deforestation were as bad as in our worst projections', reported Juan Doblas, who monitors regional deforestation for the NGO Instituto Socioambiental (ISA). 'The loss of forest in the region was so out of control that for every year between 2004 and 2013 – except 2005 – while deforestation in Amazonia as a whole fell, it increased in the region around the BR-163'. Márcio Santilli, who helped to found ISA, has worked out that 80 per cent of deforestation in the Amazon occurs within 30 kilometres (18 miles) of a paved road (Santilli, 2017). What is happening around the BR-163 is just an extreme form of what occurs along all paved roads, he explained.

Local people, too, have suffered. Pará state Environment Secretary José Alberto Colares warned in 2012 that the go-ahead was being given to construct ports and terminals in Miritituba before the necessary preparatory work had been undertaken. 'The area doesn't have any of the infrastructure it needs to deal with the social, economic, and environmental impacts', he said. 'It needs traffic controls on the roads and the river, energy transmission, public safety measures, sanitation, health, education, risk assessment, training courses, rubbish collection, water supply'. This requires significant investment, he said, and the companies shouldn't expect all the work to be done by the state (SEMAS, 2012).

Little attention seems to have been paid to the environment secretary's plea. There are 26 transhipment terminals now planned for Miritituba, with few of the necessary ancillary support services included in the investment plans. In February 2016, the Federal and State Public Ministries, independent branches of the Brazilian government, went to court to demand that three of the functioning terminals in Miritituba cease operation, partly because of the inadequacy of social and environmental impact studies. The case has not yet been heard.

Some local people have stood up for their rights and won, at least for now. A big port at Santarém might still be under construction today were it not for the opposition of *quilombola* families (descendants of runaway slaves). The National Waterway Transportation Agency (ANTAQ) was planning to build a big grain terminal beside the lake of Maicá, on the Amazon river, quite close to Santarém. Remarkably, even though there are seven *quilombola* communities located less than five kilometers (three miles) from the planned complex, environmental impact studies ignored the settlements, stating that 'no *quilombola* territory exists in the area directly affected by the project' (Locatelli, 2016). The communities mobilised and turned to the Public Ministries, demanding their right to be consulted. The Federal and State Public Ministries (see Chapter 2) went to court, asking that the port licence be suspended. In April 2016, a federal judge ruled in favour of the *quilombolas*, and work on the project stopped.

Re-engineering the river basin

Extensive though the transportation infrastructure has become in the heart of the Amazon, the multinational commodity companies and the Pará state government have hugely ambitious plans for it to be expanded even further. According to recent projections by SETRAN, the Pará Transport Secretariat, by 2026 Miritituba will be able to handle 32 million tons of grain per year, which is more than current soya bean production of the whole of the state of Mato Grosso (Salamão, 2016). But by then Mato Grosso may well be producing much more: 'It will be easy to increase [the state's] soya production to 68 million tons by 2022, provided we are given conditions in which

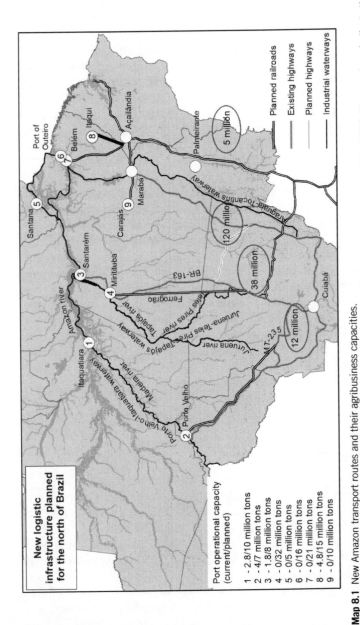

Map 8.1 New Amazon transport routes and their agribusiness capacities.
Note: The encircled numbers indicate the predicted volume of exports crops (mainly soya) expected by 2030. The numbers indicate the ports' current and future handling capacities, in tons, after planned investment.
Source: Presentation by Cargill and SETRAN-PA, 26 February 2016

we can compete', a confident Carlos Henrique Fávaro, vice-governor of Mato Grosso and soya farmer in Lucas do Rio Verde, told *Dinheiro Rural* (Santos, 2015).

To carry all these commodities, a new railway, called *Ferrogrão* (Railgrain) – running from Sinop in Mato Grosso to Miritituba – has been announced. Costing R$12.9 bn (US$4.1 bn), it will be 933 kilometres (580 miles) long and have an annual handling capacity of 36 million tons of grain. If completed in 2024, as intended, *Ferrogrão* will provide cheaper freight transport and will remove significant truck traffic from the BR-163, which is already clogged at peak times of year.

There is more: to ease the pressure on the roads yet further, the agribusiness lobby wants to transform the Juruena, Teles Pires, and Tapajós rivers into a 1,000-mile-long industrial waterway, allowing Mato Grosso soya and other crops to be containerised and transported by barge downstream all the way to the Atlantic. Key to the viability of the industrialised waterway is the building of dams and the deepening of the rivers – dynamiting waterfalls and rapids and carrying out other high-impact construction – to create a long series of navigable reservoirs. In the more distant future, an ambitious 3,300-mile railway has been proposed, to be built over the Andes to the Peruvian port of Ilo. Although the final route has not been decided, this railway, to be funded by the Chinese, is likely to run from the newly constructed port of Açu in Maranhão, through Mato Grosso, Rondônia, and Acre to the Peruvian border. Of course, as transport options multiply, so will the demand for more land to grow even more soya and maize, placing even more pressure on the environment and habitat.

Degrading the rainforest and its communities

This pressure is already being felt. Dr Wanderlei Pignati, a lecturer at the Federal University of Mato Grosso and author of several studies on pesticide health and environmental effects, told us that about 200 million litres of agrochemicals are dumped annually on Mato Grosso crops. These applications, he said, can cause 'cancer, foetal malformations, endocrine disruptions, neurological diseases, mental disorders, respiratory and intestinal disorders'.

Another problem is that studies that quantify degraded rainforest areas only measure acreage; they don't take into account traditional communities, or even indigenous lands, unless the latter have been officially demarcated – something Brazil's government has failed to accomplish in many areas. For this reason, indigenous and traditional lands are sometimes classified as places where soya is free to expand. This has led to injustices, say experts, with local communities suffering grave impacts, as agribusiness targets their lands.

Many indigenous, peasant, and traditional communities carefully clear forested areas, use them for a time, and then allow the land to recover, without destroying biodiversity. These traditional ways of occupying the land were developed over centuries and represent highly successful, sustainable methods of agroforestry management. However, the areas the people leave fallow, and to which they plan to return, are being counted as cleared areas, and thus available for agribusiness.

Rural worker and union leader Maria Ivete Bastos lives in one such community. She told us: 'Soya took over a large territory of ours, where we cultivated our crops. Little people can't fight big people, so we had to hand much of our land over. In some cases, we sold all of it, just keeping a little plot around the house'. Ivete complains about pollution from neighbouring soya plantations: 'The people who live on the plateau have creeks on their land, and they use the water from them.... All this water has become contaminated because of run-off of the pesticides they use on their soya plantations'.

Another rural worker, Dona Maria Alba Pinto de Souza, despaired: 'All my life now is in the middle of soya beans, soya farmers. They plant their soya, and it's bad for us, because you can't even rear animals'. The soya farmers want her to leave, she said: 'They've tried three times to buy my plot but I don't want to sell it'. Dona Maria believes that if she sells her land, she'll be left 'lying flat on the ground, going hungry, having nothing to eat but bread and coffee. I know many people who sold their land and now live in Santarém, with nothing. They don't have a job. Their sons live on the edge of society, their daughters end up as prostitutes. If I sell my land, I'll have to live under a bridge'.

Can the Amazon rainforest, and the world, survive this massive Amazon agribusiness onslaught? Perhaps the most ominous warning of dangerous unforeseen consequences comes from renowned Amazon scientist Tom Lovejoy, interviewed in August 2016 by *Science*, the journal of the American Association for the Advancement of Science. When asked what he considered the greatest threat to the Amazon, Lovejoy responded: The intersection between uncoordinated infra-structure and the hydrological cycle. The Amazon makes half of its own rainfall [through evapotranspiration], and the water recycles five or six times as it crosses the basin. [Deforestation disrupts] the hydrological cycle [and] is going to have effects on the weather system. With the droughts of 2005, 2010, and the current one [in 2016] – I think we're seeing flickers of the potential tipping point (Fraser 2016).

With the Amazon approaching this climate change tipping point, the much-celebrated lungs of the world are no longer working as a carbon sink – absorbing large amounts of greenhouse gases – and the region is instead becoming a carbon source, as the dying rainforest exhales its carbon into the atmosphere with in torrents potentially disastrous results for the planet (Asher, 2016). While no one knows with certainty where this deforestation tipping point lies – when somewhere between 20 and 40 per cent of the forest has been felled, scientists like Lovejoy guess – the building of dozens of roads, dams, and ports in the Tapajós, along with the resultant forest loss, pushes the basin toward that invisible point of no return (Sainsbury, 2016). With such a catastrophe looming just ahead, critics question the rush to develop the Tapajós basin as a commodities transportation corridor at the expense of the Amazon's environment, its irreplaceable biodiversity, and its indigenous and traditional inhabitants.

But surely the expansion of soya into the Amazon can be made compatible with environmental conservation? Abroad, many NGOs and environmentalists talk proudly of the Soya Moratorium, which, they say, is ensuring that tropical forest is not felled to make way for soya. It is time we took a closer look.

References

All web references were checked and still available in June/July 2018 unless otherwise stated.

Amazônia Notícias e Informação (2013) 'Megainvestimento abre nova rota para soja', [website] <http://amazonia.org.br/2013/01/megainvestimento-abre-nova-rota-para-soja/>

Asher, C. (2016) 'Study: Drought impedes tree growth, shuts down Amazon carbon sink', *Mongabay* [Website] <https://news.mongabay.com/2016/07/study-drought-impedes-tree-growth-shuts-down-amazon-carbon-sink/>

Brasiliense, R. (2004) 'Zona de impacto', *O Eco* [Website] <http://www.oeco.org.br/reportagens/793-oeco_10000/>.

Fraser, B. (2016) 'Q&A: Amazon "tipping point" may be closer than we think, Thomas Lovejoy says', *Science* [Website] <http://www.

sciencemag.org/news/2016/08/qa-amazon-tipping-point-may-be-closer-we-think-thomas-lovejoy-says>

Freitas Jr., G. and Wilson, J. (2014) 'Amazon river soy route seen extending Brazil lead on U.S.', *Bloomberg* [Website] <https://www.bloomberg.com/news/articles/2014-01-10/amazon-soy-route-seen-extending-brazil-lead-on-u-s-commodities>

Locatelli, P. (2016) 'O quilombo que parou um porto', *Repórter Brasil* [Website] <http://reporterbrasil.org.br/2016/06/o-quilombo-que-parou-um-porto/>

Oils & Fats International (2016) 'Amaggi to buy 50% of Bunge's Miritituba-Bacarena port complex', *Oils & Fats International* [Article] <http://www.ofimagazine.com/news/amaggi-to-buy-50-of-bunges-miritituba-barcarena-port-complex>

Sainsbury, C. (2016) 'Top scientists: Amazon's Tapajós dam complex "a crisis in the making"', *Mongabay* [Website] <https://news.mongabay.com/2016/11/top-scientists-amazons-tapajos-dam-complex-a-crisis-in-the-making/>

Salomão, R. (2016) 'Mato Grosso deve recuperar produtividade de soja em 2016/2017, diz IMEA', *Globorural* [Website] <http://revistagloborural.globo.com/Noticias/Agricultura/Soja/noticia/2016/08/mato-grosso-deve-recuperar-produtividade-de-soja-em-20162017-diz-imea.html>

Santilli, M. (2017) 'Amazônia esquartejada", *Folha de S. Paulo* <http://www1.folha.uol.com.br/opiniao/2017/02/1857957-amazonia-esquartejada.shtml>

Santos, B. (2015) 'Entrevista com Carlos Henrique Fávaro, vice-governador de Mato Grosso', *Dinheiro Rural* [Website] <https://www.dinheirorural.com.br/secao/entrevista/carlos-henrique-favaro-vice-governador-de-mato-grosso>

SEMAS (2012) 'Plano emergencial de prevenção a impactos sociais na zona portuária de Miritituba', *SEMAS* <https://www.semas.pa.gov.br/2012/10/22/9193/>

CHAPTER 9

Why the 'Amazon Soya Moratorium' is greenwash

Grain companies and agribusiness have widely publicised the idea that the Amazon Soya Moratorium (ASM) that they negotiated in 2006 has been a great success, pointing to the fact that direct deforestation of the Amazon biome to plant soya has declined greatly. But a closer examination shows that farmers found a way around the ASM, including the diversion of much of their new soya cultivation to the Cerrado, which is not covered by the moratorium. The ASM is essentially greenwash.

As we saw in the previous chapter, a juggernaut of expanding soya production moved into the Brazilian rainforest at the turn of the 21st century, putting a relentless squeeze on the Amazon. Soya growers arrived from the south, moving first into Mato Grosso, then leapfrogging over much of Pará to the Santarém district, with its flat plateau – ideal for agribusiness. Brazilian social movements sounded the alarm. They were justifiably worried that soya would destroy the Amazon biome along with rainforest livelihoods. On May Day 2004, protesters – acting in unison with labour movement protests across Brazil – held a large demonstration in Santarém at the new grain terminal owned by Cargill, the largest US grain trader. Joined by the international environmental NGO Greenpeace, the anti-soya offensive became urgent: Amazon deforestation was exploding. In 2003–4, annual Amazon forest loss topped 27,000 square kilometres (Carvalho et al., 2016).

An international appeal

In 2006, Greenpeace published a hard-hitting report called *Eating Up the Amazon*, showing that soya had become a serious driver of deforestation. The NGO accused fast-food restaurants, supermarkets, and agribusiness of forest crime for their failure to responsibly manage the 4,000-mile soya supply chain that started with the clearing of virgin Amazon forest and ended in US poultry, pork, and beef feedlots and on American and European dinner plates (Greenpeace, 2006). The story resonated with the international press (Vidal, 2006).

Photo 9.1 There is a staggering loss of biodiversity when rainforest is converted to soya.
Photo by Mayangdi Inzaulgarat

McDonalds, Walmart, and other big transnational food corporations sought a way to shine up a tarnished public image. In a hasty attempt at damage control, they contacted the big grain traders, including Cargill and Bunge, and began talks with Greenpeace. The result: the Amazon Soya Moratorium (ASM), the first major voluntary zero-deforestation agreement reached in the tropics. In the pact, nine out of ten companies in the Brazilian soya market agreed not to purchase soya grown on land within the Amazon biome deforested after 2006, and also to blacklist farmers using slave labour.

Even before the moratorium was signed, however, the annual rate of Amazon deforestation fell dramatically, by almost 50 per cent. It was hard to see how the ASM could have caused this remarkable decline but, even so, it was touted as being responsible, with the Ethical Consumer calling the moratorium 'an incredible success' (Ethical Consumer, 2016) and Cargill describing it in its advertising as 'a resounding success' (Schraeder, 2015). This reported achievement led to multiple renewals, and in 2016 the soya industry agreed to make the ASM permanent (Butler, 2009a). The only major change over time was a shift in baseline, originally fixed at 2006, then moved to 2008 to fit with the government's controversial 2012 forest code (Woods Hole Research Center, 2014).

The question today: has the ASM truly played a key role in stemming Amazon deforestation, and was it even designed to achieve that result? Or has it largely served as an industry PR tool that distracts

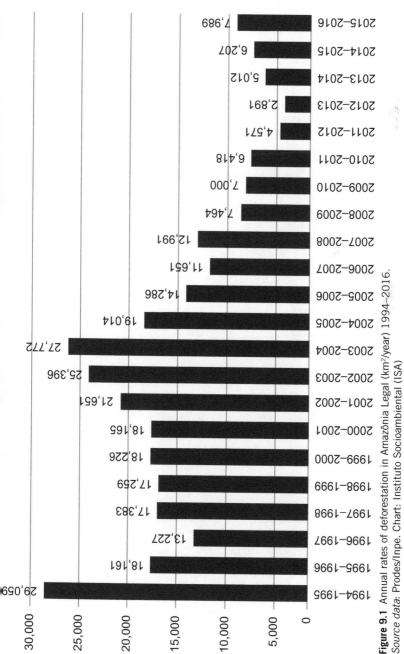

Figure 9.1 Annual rates of deforestation in Amazônia Legal (km²/year) 1994–2016.
Source data: Prodes/Inpe. Chart: Instituto Socioambiental (ISA)

global consumers from the environmental and social harm being done by large-scale Brazilian soya plantations?

Measuring the moratorium

In 2014, scientists decided to thoroughly investigate the ASM's overall effectiveness. University of Wisconsin–Madison Assistant Professor of Geography Holly Gibbs and her team published the results in the prestigious academic journal *Science* in January 2015:

> In the two years preceding the agreement, nearly 30 per cent of soy expansion [in the Amazon biome] occurred through deforestation rather than by replacement of pasture or other previously cleared lands. After the Soy [Moratorium], deforestation for soy dramatically decreased, falling to only 1 per cent of expansion in the Amazon biome by 2014 (Gibbs et al., 2015).

This appears to be an unambiguous vindication of the moratorium. But not necessarily. The study points out that many farmers in Mato Grosso, who were responsible for 85 per cent of the soya planted in the Amazon biome, were continuing to clear forest illegally on their land while claiming compliance with the ASM:

> At least 627 soy properties in Mato Grosso violated the FC [Brazil's forest code] and cleared forest illegally during the Soy [Moratorium]. Yet only 115 properties were excluded by soy traders for Soy [Moratorium] violations. This discrepancy can occur because the Soy [Moratorium] regulates only the portion of the property where soy is grown – not the entire property (Gibbs et al., 2015).

In other words, farmers can be hacking down forest on their property but, provided they don't plant this cleared area with soya, they are not infringing the moratorium. This loophole compromised the effectiveness of the ASM, yet no mention of it was ever made in the pro-ASM promotional materials circulated by moratorium advocates.

It is true that Amazon deforestation fell dramatically during most of the early years of the moratorium. So what caused this decline, if not the ASM? A study published by *Science* in 2014 found that at least three factors accounted for the reduction, with the ASM regarded as the least important of them. In an interview with us, Earth Innovation Institute Director and Lead Researcher Dan Nepstad cautioned: 'It is impossible to quantify exactly the effect of the moratorium on deforestation. I think it was responsible for 5–10 per cent of the total decline'.

Two other factors had bigger impacts, his team found. By 2004, so much Amazon forest had been cleared that there was plenty of land for agribusiness expansion, and using this already cleared land didn't violate the ASM. The second factor related to 'improvements in livestock yields, which had further reduced the demand for new land to be cleared'. In other words, there was less need than in the past to clear land to plant pasture – generally the primary driver of deforestation.

In evaluating the overall effectiveness of the ASM, it is very important to look at exactly what it achieved. Gibbs' team were extremely careful in their 2015 study's conclusion, saying that: 'deforestation for soy dramatically decreased', without, it should be noted, crediting the ASM for the fall. NGOs and some in the press were not so meticulous. Greenpeace, for example, claimed that the moratorium represented 'a huge step towards halting Amazon deforestation' (Greenpeace, 2009). This statement is not accurate: what the moratorium set out to do, and largely achieved, was to stop Amazon forest being directly cleared to plant soya. However, this is very different from halting deforestation in the Amazon. The studies suggest that, to a large extent, the decline in deforestation in the post-ASM period was not the result of the moratorium.

Gaming the moratorium

The hard truth is that, if deforestation of the Amazon biome is to be stopped, farmers need to stop felling forest, even when their farming activities, as practised today, require more land. And there is nothing to suggest that this happened. For there are many ways in which forest can be cleared without violating the ASM. One, described by Gibbs and already mentioned, was simply for farmers to clear forest in other parts of their property and to make sure they planted pasture or other crops, but not soya, on this land. Another similar ploy is to plant soya on pasture lands cleared before 2008, which is permitted under the ASM. But the displaced cattle now require new pasture, which the farmers may create themselves by clearing land or they may purchase from land thieves, who lay waste the rainforest, often driving out indigenous and traditional people, and then sell the cleared land to ranchers. None of this is banned by the ASM.

Bernardo Machado Pires, who manages environmental issues for the Brazilian Association of the Vegetable Oil Industries, (ABIOVE, Associação Brasileira das Indústrias de Óleos Vegetais), believes that this second wheeze is very common. 'Very often the cultivation of soya moves to areas where cattle are reared and the cattle move into the forest', he said. 'And the soya industry is indirectly responsible for this'. Research conducted in 2006 by Dan Nepstad reached a similar conclusion: 'In my interviews with farmers in Mato Grosso, several spoke about the way cattle producers (and land thieves) get capital by selling their land to soya farmers', he told us (Terra, 2013).

Greenpeace became aware of this cattle loophole and helped to negotiate a deal with Brazil's three largest meatpacking firms, who agreed not to purchase cattle reared on illegally cleared Amazon forest lands or from properties using slave labour (Butler, 2009b). But Brazilian farmers are nothing if not ingenious, and it seems that this agreement, too, is often infringed. When we were in the district of Castelo de Sonhos in 2014, employees from Brazil's largest meat-packing company, JBS, told us that the meatpacking firms themselves had found ways of getting round the deal. The most widespread, they said, is 'cattle laundering', by which cattle owners move cattle that were reared on illegally cleared land onto established pastures just before they are slaughtered.

Of course, large-scale soya production indirectly drives Amazon deforestation in yet another, indirect way: new and improved roads, such as highway BR-163, lobbied for by soya growers, and built primarily to move soya from Brazil's interior to market, give large numbers of illegal loggers, land grabbers, and ranchers access to the new areas of virgin forest. Commodities companies Cargill, Bunge, and Amaggi (Brazil's largest soya producer) are also committed to a massive soya transport infrastructure expansion that would traverse the heart of the Brazilian Amazon, helping to deforest the Tapajós basin, bringing new roads, railways, and an industrial waterway, along with 40-plus major dams.

So has the moratorium been effective? Antônio Ioris, Senior Lecturer of Human Geography at Cardiff University and author of a book on Mato Grosso agribusiness, says not. In his view, it has actually been counter-productive: 'The moratorium obfuscates the debate', Ioris told us. 'Its main objective is to improve the image of the agribusiness sector and to reduce somewhat the stigma of soya production being an activity with highly negative environmental and social impacts.

Those who have gained most with the moratorium are agribusiness leaders, the Ministry of the Environment, and NGOs. Those who have gained least are the ecosystems and the local populations'. Yet the idea that the ASM is successful is widely accepted, especially among NGOs. In her otherwise excellent article on the way the world's chocolate industry is driving deforestation in West Africa, Ruth Maclean calls for a moratorium on forest cleared for cacao cultivation, saying that 'the one on soya worked well in the Amazon' (Maclean, 2017).

Focusing on one while ignoring another

With so much media attention concentrated on the ASM, another serious problem – that of the destruction of Brazil's biodiverse Cerrado – has been neglected. Amazônia Legal (as defined by the Brazilian government) covers two biomes: the Amazon biome and part of the Cerrado biome. The ASM covers only the former. And both biomes contain plenty of room for the soya industry to expand without violating the letter of the ASM agreement. 'There still are 40.5 million hectares (156,371 square miles) of anthropised land [degraded by human activity] with a high or medium aptitude for soya – with 22 million hectares [84,942 square miles] in Amazonia and 18.5 million hectares [71,428 square miles] in the Cerrado. It is mainly occupied by pasture and it is to these lands that

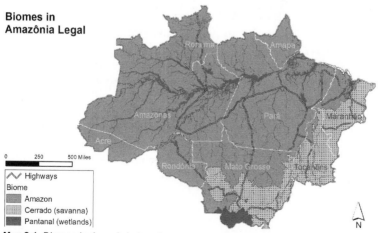

Biomes in Amazônia Legal

Map 9.1 Biomes in Amazônia Legal.
Note: Amazônia Legal includes all of the Amazon biome, plus a portion of the Cerrado biome and a tiny part of the Pantanal biome.
Map by Maurício Torres

the government must direct future grain expansion', said INPA scientist Arnaldo Carneiro, whose study looked at the possibilities of commercial agriculture expansion in the region.

Although Carneiro's work, along with other agribusiness-backed studies, claims this vast acreage as a 'sustainable' solution to the industry's need for new croplands, this doesn't mean that all of it is readily available to large-scale farmers. Much is currently occupied by a wide variety of groups – including land thieves, cattle ranchers, peasant and traditional communities, and agrarian reform settlements. Some of this land may be occupied in a sustainable way by traditional communities, and should not have been classified as 'anthropised' in the sense of being degraded. It is a complex issue, and there could well be a great deal of conflict, especially in the Amazon biome, before the destiny of this land is decided. Adding to the complications, some of this 'available' land in the Amazon biome will have been cleared after 2008 and, on paper at least, is banned for soya use by the ASM.

But, as the Cerrado isn't covered by the moratorium, this region is up for grabs for agribusiness: even if it was cultivated on recently cleared land, all soya produced there can be marketed with the ASM-compliant, but false, claim that it caused 'zero deforestation in the productive chain'. And unfortunately for Brazil, the world, and wildlife living there, the Cerrado is one of the planet's richest tropical savannah regions, with high levels of endemism. But that biodiversity is rapidly vanishing. Researchers recently used satellite data to show that Cerrado cropland within a 45-million hectare area in Matopiba (an acronym for the parts of the states of Maranhão, Tocantins, Piauí, and Bahia located in the Cerrado) doubled in recent years, increasing from 1.3 million hectares in 2003 to 2.5 million hectares in 2013 (Gaworecki, 2016). The researchers found that almost three-quarters of this agricultural expansion was achieved through the destruction of native Cerrado vegetation. 'This is the first study to show how intense deforestation and agricultural expansion in the Cerrado have been in the past decade', the University of Vermont's Gillian Galford, a co-author of the study, said in a statement. 'It's clearly a new hotspot for tropical deforestation' (Jokhai, 2016).

Experts have seriously questioned the wisdom of placing so much emphasis through the ASM on the damage done exclusively to tropical forests. In 2015, Gibbs called for the ASM to be extended to the Cerrado: 'If large-scale soy expansion continues in Matopiba, remaining natural vegetation could be highly susceptible to soy conversion without additional safeguards. Expanding the Soy [Moratorium] could reduce the ongoing direct conversion of Cerrado vegetation to soy' (Gibbs et al., 2015). But this has not happened yet. Brazil's environment minister, José Sarney Filho, suggested last year that the moratorium be extended to the Cerrado, and talks began, said Tica Minami, leader of Greenpeace Brazil's Amazon Project. But no deal has been struck, largely because the soya industry is reportedly very reluctant to come on board.

Meanwhile, soya expansion continues at full throttle there. Mighty Earth, a global environmental organisation, recently sent researchers into the region (Bellantonio et al., n.d.). They travelled for hundreds of miles in the Cerrado and, to their dismay, always found the same: 'Vast areas of savannah recently converted to enormous soybean monocultures that stretch to the horizon'. Farmers confirmed to Mighty Earth that they are selling mainly to Cargill and Bunge – two leading ASM signatories – with these companies often providing the financial incentives that are fuelling the savannah's transformation.

The Mighty Earth report urges a moratorium: 'The kind of deforestation we found in the Cerrado ... is not inevitable. In the Brazilian Amazon, Cargill, Bunge, and other companies have figured out how to protect ecosystems and still grow their businesses'. This is dangerous talk, further propagating the myth that the ASM was highly successful and that it is possible for agribusiness to continue expanding at a rapid pace and still protect the ecosystems – something we would strongly dispute.

The ASM has worked in the Amazon biome only because there was already so much cleared land there and agribusiness could move into the ASM-excluded Cerrado lands without infringing the moratorium. This has allowed the companies to publicise their success in protecting the forest without essentially changing the way they operate. While Cargill is destroying the Cerrado, it can use the ASM to cover itself with an aura of green sustainability, stating on its website:

> In Brazil, we have seen great progress as we partnered to advance the soy moratorium in the Amazon for more than a decade. Today, we are working with more than 15,000 soy farmers and collaborating with governments, NGOs and partners to

implement the Brazilian forest code and advance forest protection' (Cargill, n.d.).

In 2015, Cargill, Greenpeace, and McDonalds were jointly awarded the Keystone Prize for 'leadership in significantly reducing deforestation' (Saccone, 2015).

Soya moratorium or greenwash?

The underlying conundrum – as shown in earlier chapters – is that mechanised soya production on the gigantic industrial scale pursued in Brazil leads to dramatic wholesale changes in land use and destroys biodiversity. It concentrates land ownership in the hands of the wealthy few while exacerbating social inequality and failing to tackle poverty. It simply is not compatible with the conservation of the forest and the people who live in it. The ASM addresses a single narrow aspect of soya production – direct deforestation for soya cultivation in the Amazon biome – but ignores other far graver concerns, which, indeed, were never in its brief.

In response, soya moratorium defenders point to the Amazonian deforestation the ASM managed to prevent, and note that the moratorium became the model for zero deforestation commitments in the global palm oil, pulp and paper, and rubber sectors as well as helping to shape the Brazilian cattle agreement. This is true but also very limited. What is dangerous about the ASM is that it allows its advocates to make wildly overblown claims, with Greenpeace even previously presenting it as 'a game changer for the Amazon' and 'one of the best examples of how zero deforestation can be put into practice and proof that ending the destruction of the Amazon is beneficial for everyone, including industry' (Branford and Torres, 2017).

This is an inaccurate and misleading claim: it distracts global attention away from the very serious problems created by soya; it obscures the inherent contradiction between the rapid expansion of agribusiness and the preservation of the forest and its people; and, by providing the soya industry with extremely useful propaganda, it empowers a sector that is causing widespread environmental and social devastation. Essentially the ASM is greenwash.

Time, we felt, to leave the debate over soya and start travelling north along the BR-163 highway, moving from the 'tamed' region around the towns of Sorriso and Sinop, where agribusiness has won, to the north, where the battle over who is to control the land is still being fought.

Response from Greenpeace Brazil

This response was appended to the authors' original article on Mongabay (Branford and Torres, 2017).

> Mongabay's recent article (Branford and Torres, 2017) correctly identifies several major impacts from industrial soya production that are not prevented by the Amazon Soy Moratorium. The Moratorium only covers deforestation linked with soy and slave labour in the Amazon and it does not have the scope to address every problem related to the existing agribusiness model in South America such as agrochemicals, land ownership concentration, or land conflicts.
>
> Acknowledging the agreement's limitations, Greenpeace cannot agree on the moratorium being dismissed as 'greenwash'. The moratorium has produced objectively measured results and represents a genuine investment of resources on the part of NGOs, the soya industry, financial institutions, soya customers, and the Brazilian Government. One of those results is that there are at least 8 million hectares of Amazon rainforest which have not been converted to soya plantations despite them being suitable for crop production and lacking any official protection (such as being designated conservation units, indigenous peoples' lands, or even agrarian settlements).
>
> The Moratorium continues to present a major step in halting Amazon deforestation as it has effectively contained a significant driver. In previous years, about 30 to 40 per cent of the deforested areas were converted directly to soya plantations and today this number represents just over 1 per cent. The Moratorium is one of the many steps needed to reach zero deforestation. Other necessary pieces of this puzzle still need to materialize fully such as: honouring the rights of indigenous peoples and other traditional forest communities, responsible finance, conservation funding, improved monitoring and enforcement, a zero deforestation law, limits on infrastructure development, and containment of other deforestation drivers such as cattle.
>
> The Moratorium is a bona fide solution that presented a significant mind-shift, being the first voluntary zero deforestation commitment. Nonetheless it would be inappropriate for any company involved to utilize its successes on soya to divert

attention from other controversies or other geographies, such as Cerrado. Greenpeace is a supporter of the soya moratorium as an effective platform to halt deforestation and, at the same time, has an active agriculture campaign globally in response to the failed industrial agribusiness model. In Brazil, this agriculture campaign promotes agroecology and has been very critical of the use of agrochemicals (Branford and Torres, 2017).

References

All web references were checked and still available in June/July 2018 unless otherwise stated.

Bellantonio, M., Hurowitz, G., Gronlund, A.L. and Yousefi, A. (no date) 'The ultimate mystery meat – Exposing the secrets behind Burger King and global meat production', *RFN and Mighty Meat* [Website] <http://www.mightyearth.org/mysterymeat/>

Branford, S. and Torres, M. (2017) 'Amazon soy moratorium: defeating deforestation or greenwash diversion?', *Mongabay* [Website] <https://news.mongabay.com/2017/03/amazon-soy-moratorium-defeating-deforestation-or-greenwash-diversion/>

Butler, R. (2009a) 'Rainforest soy moratorium shows success in the Brazilian Amazon', *Mongabay* [Website] <https://news.mongabay.com/2009/04/rainforest-soy-moratorium-shows-success-in-the-brazilian-amazon/>

Butler, R. (2009b) 'Brazilian beef giants agree to moratorium on Amazon deforestation', *Mongabay* [Website] <https://news.mongabay.com/2009/10/brazilian-beef-giants-agree-to-moratorium-on-amazon-deforestation/>

Cargill (no date) 'Sustainable soy in Brazil – reducing deforestation in the Amazon', *Cargill* [Website] <https://www.cargill.com/sustainability/soy/sustainable-soy-in-brazil>

Carvalho, T.S., Magalhães, A.S. and Domingues, E.P. (2016) 'Desmatamento e a contribuição econômica da floresta na Amazônia', *Estudos Econômicos (São Paulo)* 46(2) <http://www.scielo.br/scielo.php?script=sci_arttext&pid=S0101-41612016000200499>

Ethical Consumer (2016) 'Is soya sustainable?' *Ethical Consumer* [online] <http://www.ethicalconsumer.org/commentanalysis/environment/soyaanddeforestation.aspx>

Gaworecki, M. (2016) 'Brazil's Cerrado region: a new tropical deforestation hotpot', *Mongabay* [Website] <https://news.mongabay.com/2016/04/brazils-CERRADO-region-a-new-tropical-deforestation-hotspot/>

Gibbs, H.K., Rausch, L., Muger, J., Schelly, I., Morton, D.C., Noojipady, P., Soares-Filho, B., Barreto, P., Micol, L. and Walker, N.F. (2015) 'Brazil's soy moratorium – supply-chain governance is needed to avoid deforestation', *Science* 347(6220): 377–8 <https://nelson.wisc.edu/sage/docs/publications/GibbsetalScience2015.pdf>

Greenpeace (2006) 'Eating up the Amazon' *Greenpeace* [Website] <http://www.greenpeace.org/international/Global/international/planet-2/report/2006/7/eating-up-the-amazon.pdf>

Greenpeace (2009) 'Soya Moratorium', *Greenpeace* [Websites] <http://www.greenpeace.org/international/en/campaigns/forests/amazon/threats-and-solutions/soya-moratorium/>

Jokhai, R. (2016) 'Agricultural expansion depletes natural areas', *The John Hopkins Newsletter* [Website] <http://www.jhunewsletter.com/2016/04/14/agricultural-expansion-depletes-natural-areas/>

Maclean, R. (2017) 'Chocolate industry drives rainforest disaster in Ivory Coast', *The Guardian* [Website] <https://www.theguardian.com/environment/2017/sep/13/chocolate-industry-drives-rainforest-disaster-in-ivory-coast>

Saccone, M. (2015) 'Keystone Policy Center honors national leaders in energy, education, environment, public policy', *TNTP* <https://tntp.org/news-and-press/view/keystone-policy-center-honors-national-leaders-in-energy-education-environm>

Schraeder, C. (2015) 'Stronger when we work together: lessons from the Brazilian soy moratorium', *Cargill* <https://www.cargill.com/story/stronger-working-together-lessons-from-brazilian-soy-moratorium >

Terra (2013) 'Soja é responsável indireta pelo desmatamento no Brasil', 17 September 2013 <https://www.terra.com.br/noticias/ciencia/sustentabilidade/soja-e-responsavel-indireta-pelo-desmatamento-no-brasil,3febd717c9c21410VgnCLD2000000ec6eb0aRCRD.html>

Vidal, J. (2006) 'The 7,000km journey that links Amazon destruction to fast food', *The Guardian* [Website] <https://www.theguardian.com/business/2006/apr/06/brazil.food>

Woods Hole Research Center (2014) 'Untangling Brazil's controversial new forest code', [Website] <https://www.sciencedaily.com/releases/2014/04/140424143735.htm>

CHAPTER 10
All crime and no punishment

One of the most notorious land grabbers operating beside the BR-163 highway in the south of Pará state is AJ Vilela, from a wealthy São Paulo family. Like his father, he has evicted peasant families, using threats and violence. For years they have acted with impunity but, in 2016, he and his sister were arrested as a result of a police operation known as Flying Rivers. While this in itself is unprecedented, as yet the authorities have not confiscated their land. Impunity is still alive and well.

Every month, a group of wealthy women, representing some of Brazil's most exclusive and powerful land-owning families, meets in São Paulo at the Brazilian Rural Society. One of the leading lights of the 23 'ladies of agribusiness', as they're known, used to be a glamorous socialite named Ana Luiza Junqueira Vilela Viacava, who often featured in Brazil's *Vogue* magazine. In 2012, she declared: 'I like land and the security it gives me for the future' (Ondei, n.d.).

In July 2016, Ana Luiza was arrested and charged with land grabbing. An unflattering picture of her startled face, taken by the police after her detention, appeared in the national press. She was charged as part of Operation Flying Rivers (*Operação Rios Voadores*), a well-planned, well-coordinated law enforcement action launched in June of 2016 by several arms of the Brazilian government. Its objective: to dismantle a powerful gang of land thieves who had illegally occupied and deforested huge tracts of public land near Castelo dos Sonhos, a town on Brazil's BR-163 highway in Pará state. Heading the gang of Amazon land grabbers was Ana Luiza's brother, 39-year-old Antônio José Junqueira Vilela Filho, known as AJ Vilela, or Jotinha. The gang's number two was Anna Luiza's husband, Ricardo Caldeira Viacava.

The band had been operating for years and had illegally cleared 300 square kilometres of forest, an area five times the size of New York's Manhattan Island. It was all public land. This made AJ Vilela 'the largest individual clearer of land in the Amazon since the monitoring of deforestation began', according to Juan Doblas, one of the authors of a recently published book about land grabbing and deforestation called *Dono é quem desmata*, which translates as 'He who clears the land owns it'

(Torres et al., 2017). It took two years of careful investigation to bring Operation Flying Rivers to fruition. It mobilised 95 federal police, 15 tax experts, and 32 employees from IBAMA, Brazil's federal environment agency. Authorisation was given to tap phones and to hack into bank accounts, and the operation was launched on 30 June 2016, when 24 federal arrest warrants were issued.

At first, Ana Luiza was required only to give a police statement – an order not enforced as she was on holiday in the USA. However, in the days following the initial bust, police wiretaps showed that she was making calls from outside the country, urging people in Brazil to destroy or hide evidence that could incriminate her brother, who was still at large, her husband, who was already in prison, and other gang members. When she landed in Guarulhos Airport in São Paulo on 4 July 2016, she was arrested. A few days later, her brother, who had gone into hiding, gave himself up.

AJ Vilela and Ana Luíza are the offspring of Antônio José Rossi Junqueira Vilela, known as AJJ, a prominent, wealthy cattle rancher whose achievements as a breeder of Nelore cattle have long been praised in the nation's agribusiness media (MF Rural, 2012). One influential magazine acclaimed him as 'a model of success from whom large and small ranchers can learn lessons' (Dinheiro Rural, 2011).

Photo 10.1 AJ Vilela, who holds the record for the largest fines ever imposed on an individual by IBAMA for environmental crimes.
Photo by ver-o-fato.com.br

AJJ saw to it that his children achieved celebrity status, with photos of AJ Vilela and Ana Luíza often appearing in Brazil's most exclusive social columns – posing and smiling at private art exhibit openings and exclusive fashion shows, rubbing shoulders with the elite. A high point of 2013's social calendar, for example, was an extravaganza celebrating AJ Vilela's 35th birthday at his luxury home in Jardim Europa, one of São Paulo's most exclusive neighbourhoods (Glamurama, 2013).

In 2010, AJ Vilela travelled to the tiny Caribbean island of Saint Barths to marry Ana Khouri, a fashionable Brazilian jewellery designer, whose work adorns Madonna and other celebrities. On her website, Ana Khouri attests to using only Fair Trade gold in her work, of buying from mines 'run according to exacting social, economic, and environmental regulations that protect workers, their families, and entire communities', and of not contributing 'to abuse through conflict, enslavement, and child labour'. Her international customers, and probably even Ana Khouri herself, almost certainly had no idea that her former husband – they separated in 2012 – was illegally clearing land in the Amazon as far back as 2010, and illegally appropriating and deforesting public lands to create cattle pasture as recently as 2016, while keeping workers in conditions analogous to slavery. Nor would they probably have been aware that the wealth boasted by AJ Vilela arose from unsavoury business activities conducted near the impoverished, remote Amazonian town of Castelo dos Sonhos, a world away from the rich, well-connected surroundings of São Paulo's Jardim Europa.

A dynasty of fortune hunters

To unravel and understand AJ Vilela's criminal history, we need to look back at the life of his father, AJJ. As with many other self-made men in the Amazon, AJJ got his big break in Mato Grosso state in 1967 when, at the age of 20, he procured 10,000 hectares from the Brazilian authorities, who at the time were eager to push out indigenous and traditional peoples and to repopulate the Amazon with new settlers. In what was still a remote, wild, densely forested region, AJJ 'set out to achieve his dream of becoming a great and respected cattle rancher' (Dinheiro Rural, 2011).

On the way to achieving this dream, he worked for a time in the state of Rondônia in the south-west of the Amazon basin, where he took over Yvypytã Ranch. There, his name became associated with some gruesome events, though charges were never filed: in 1983, he was accused of ordering the killing of miners panning for gold on his land (Milanez, 2016); and in 1986, he was alleged to have been involved in an attempt to wipe out a group of isolated Indians, also living on his land, by poisoning them with sugar laced with arsenic (Milanez, 2010).

Back in Mato Grosso, AJJ became 'great and respected', though he openly boasted that, in his early days as a rancher, he carried out extensive deforestation: 'I bought a lot of land in Mato Grosso, when land was still cheap. I paid a symbolic amount. Something like a dollar a hectare. So I bought large areas, opened ranches, and then sold them on. During this period, I had as much as 200,000 hectares [494,210 acres]' (Dinheiro Rural, 2011). It seems that he deforested not only his own land: he was fined R$60 m (US$20 m) for clearing land within the Cristalino State Park, at the time the highest penalty ever charged by the Mato Grosso state government for an environmental crime.

But AJJ never paid the fine. More remarkably, perhaps, he still received public funding to build two small hydroelectric plants inside the park, with money coming from the Amazon Development Fund (FDA) (about R$60 m, US$19 m), the National Economic and Social Development Bank (BNDES Banco Nacional de Desenvolvimento Econômico e Social) (R$10 m, US$3 m), and Banco da Amazônia (about R$9.9 m, US$3 m). All this despite reports of irregularities in permits granted for the work, including the most obvious – the concession of a licence for a hydroelectric dam within a conservation unit (Diário de Cuiabá, 2007; Gazeta Digital, 2007).

The case was reviewed by the Parliamentary Commission of Enquiry (CPI Comissão Parlamentar de Inquérito) into small-scale hydro-projects in the Mato Grosso legislative assembly, because accusations had been made that the project licences had been obtained using false documents (Ribeiro, 2011; Teodoro, n.d.). It was reported that AJJ was an important backer of the former governor of Mato Grosso, Blairo Maggi, and that the licences had been granted as part of a political deal (Cavalcanti, 2011; Ribeiro, 2011). Today, Blairo Maggi is Brazil's agriculture minister. The construction work on the dams was halted, but AJJ's cattle went on grazing inside the park despite the lawsuits and the fines. Impunity was rife in the region but, even so, AJJ had a special knack for living safely outside the law.

Photo 10.2 IBAMA official views a tree cut by the AJ Vilela gang.
Photo by Environmental Protection Directorate of Brazil (IBAMA, Diretoria de
Proteção Ambiental)

AJ Vilela appears to have begun his illegal deforestation activities in
Pará in 2010 and 2011. IBAMA soon became aware of his clear-cutting,
imposing heavy fines and banning any further economic activity on
the cleared lands. AJ Vilela followed in his father's footsteps, and
even outdid him; today he holds the record for the largest fines ever
imposed on an individual by IBAMA for environmental crimes: a total
of R\$332,765,736.50 (US\$111 m).

He followed his father's example in another way and simply ignored
the fines. Not that they would have bankrupted him: they amounted
to not even one-fifth of the R\$1.9 bn (US\$600 m) that passed through
his bank accounts between 2012 and 2015, according to the MPF. Few
in Brazil are surprised by his failure to pay: 'Have you ever heard of
organised crime paying its fines?' responded Luciano Evaristo, IBAMA's
head of environmental protection, when asked whether AJ Vilela had
ever paid any of the huge penalties imposed on him. So again, like the
father, the son shrugged off the setbacks, opened new pastures, put cattle
on them, and went on clearing rainforest. When he was finally arrested as
part of Operation Flying Rivers, more than four years after beginning his
illegal activities – and after making it clear that he had no intention of
stopping – he had cleared 300 square kilometres of forest.

Destruction and slavery

AJ Vilela and his illegal activities left a swath of environmental and social damage. Throughout our journey to the Amazon basin in November 2016, people spoke to us of the violence with which he and his gunmen had imposed their rule of terror in the region, and of the failure of the authorities for many years to hold the gang to account. Many farmers, from small landowners to peasant families, spoke of the way people had been violently – and illegally – evicted from their land. One peasant farmer, who wanted to speak off the record for understandable reasons, told us: 'The man who was farming this land before was kicked off by brute force. It was the Vilelas who did it. They used bullets. Anyone who tried to return was killed. So people are very frightened of the Vilelas. You just have to say the name Vilela and people tremble, they shiver. Because they're barbaric'.

On one occasion, AJ Vilela was taken to court for attempted murder. He and his henchmen were accused of ambushing and firing on a rural landless worker, Dezuíta Assis Ribeiro Chagas, who was taking part in a peaceful occupation near a farm belonging to the Vilela family in Pontal do Paranapanema. According to press reports, 'the federal police recorded a conversation in which AJ Vilela's lawyer ordered him to get rid of weapons used in the crime' (Jornal Nacional, 2016). This is part of the transcript:

> Lawyer: They [AJ Vilela's gunmen] may be called in for questioning or even arrested.
>
> AJ Vilela: Okay.
>
> Lawyer: Make sure to get rid of the tools [the federal police term for weapons].

We learned that the case, which had been put on hold due to lack of evidence, was recently reopened.

In addition to accusations of land theft and deforestation, AJ Vilela and his brother-in-law, Ricardo Caldeira Viacava, have been accused of utilizing slave labour and violating labour legislation. Viacava – Ana Luíza's husband – likewise comes from a wealthy São Paulo family that made its fortune in ranching. His father, Carlos Viacava, was minister of finance during the military government of General João Baptista Figueiredo and owns large ranches. A former president of the Association of Nelore Breeders of Brazil, he was chosen by *Dinheiro Rural* magazine in 2016 as one of the 100 most influential personalities in agribusiness (CV Nelore Mocho, 2016).

IBAMA launched a separate action at the same time as Operation Flying Rivers. That investigation ended with AJ Vilela and Ricardo Viacava being accused of holding labourers, employed to clear forest, in conditions analogous to slavery. According to charges filed by the MPF, the workers 'began to clear forest at 4.30 a.m. and only stopped work at 5.30 p.m.', and were 'subjected to gruelling working hours'. Interestingly, the two men were not caught by the federal government's sophisticated system of surveillance of illegal logging, using real-time geo-monitoring, but thanks to the Kayapó Indians, an Amazonian indigenous group that has developed their own even more effective – if somewhat less high-tech – system for monitoring goings on in their territory.

Satellite images can, by their nature, record harm done to a forest only after it has occurred. Remote sensoring detects changes in vegetation cover only after a forest has been felled, when bare ground has been revealed. Then alerts are triggered and an inspection team is sent out to confirm the devastation. By then, the trees have already been cut and there is rarely any sign of the slave labour often employed to do the logging.

In 2014, a gang headed by AJ Vilela started clearing an area of 14,000 hectares on the border of the Baú Indigenous Territory, which belongs to the Kayapó Indians. His gang organised 20 camps, each with 10 workers, distributed across the area. They ran a technologically savvy operation, calculated to avoid the prying eyes of satellites. Chainsaw operators felled the understorey and some big trees, but left just the right number of large trees untouched to keep the canopy cover intact, so that the satellites failed to spot bare ground.

AJ Vilela – both a sophisticated entrepreneur and a criminal – had hired geo-monitoring whizz-kids to inform his overseers in the field precisely how many trees they could safely fell without their work being captured by the satellites. 'In this way, the system did not emit deforestation alerts and, without alerts, there was no reason for the inspectors to go to the area', explained Evaristo. When understorey clearing was complete, the remaining large trees could then be felled. Only then would the damage be seen by the satellites and, by the time IBAMA arrived in the area, the land thieves would be gone.

However, the gang underestimated the territorial monitoring capacity of the Kayapó. Evaristo told us: 'The Kayapó came to Brasília to report the terrible deforestation that was being carried out on the border of their territory and they demanded that measures be taken'. This indigenous report took the government by surprise – the

Photo 10.3 Kayapó Indians stand with an IBAMA official as chain saws and other equipment used in the illegal deforestation operation are destroyed.
Photo by Environmental Protection Directorate of Brazil (IBAMA, Diretoria de Proteção Ambiental)

geo-monitoring system wasn't registering any deforestation where the Indians said it was happening. IBAMA scrambled to send investigators in, including the director of environmental protection. 'The Indians took us directly to five camps, and there we found 44 people busy at work in conditions analogous to slavery', said Evaristo. The director was astonished at the Indians' ability to monitor the forest: 'The Indians have an efficient intelligence system, and the various villages use radio to tell each other in Kayapó what is going on', he said. 'In this way, they always know what is happening in their territory'. The discovery of slave labour in the tree-clearing camps led authorities to intensify their investigation and to broaden the sweep of the ongoing Operation Flying Rivers.

Plus ça change

AJ Vilela's father, AJJ, was never punished for his criminal activities, even though he was given very heavy fines (few of which he ever paid) and lawsuits were brought against him. Ana Luiza was freed on 20 July, after two weeks in jail (Racy, 2016). AJ Vilela was behind bars for a while longer, being released in October 2016. The whole family has disappeared from the social columns, and their court cases are ongoing. Brazilian justice is notoriously slow, and the gang has very good lawyers defending it, so no one knows when the verdict will come or what it will be.

Even so, Operation Flying Rivers achieved something important. Until recently, AJ Vilela's father (who has also disappeared from the scene and apparently suffers from Alzheimer's disease) was committing acts much like his son and boasting about it in the press. Before now, it was extremely unusual for leading figures in agribusiness to be arrested. That this has happened is in itself ground-breaking. However, the state has not reclaimed the land that AJ Vilela, Ricardo Caldeira Viacava, and their crew illegally occupied. In our visit to Pará in November 2016, we found that this land, though officially embargoed, is still recognised as belonging to them by neighbours, while men employed by the gang, we were told, are still fattening cattle on these properties.

So, as things stand, the defendants are not in jail, but await trial; they have not paid the large fines that were imposed; the embargo on land use is not being respected; most seriously, the public land that AJ Vilela illegally occupied is still firmly in his gang's hands.

In the light of this, we asked Evaristo if anything has really changed. Thanks to the embargo, he said, 'the gang will not be able to sell the cattle they have fattened on their land, because the slaughterhouses will not purchase cattle from embargoed areas'. Also, the gang will be unable to obtain legal titles to the land. But locals told us that there are easy workarounds: while the slaughterhouses have pledged not to buy cattle reared on embargoed land, it is straightforward, quick, and cheap to launder the cattle. Livestock illegally fattened in one place need simply to be taken for a short while to a legal ranch, as the slaughter-houses check only the last supplier. Federal prosecutor Patrícia Daros Xavier said that, 'there are documents that show that big slaughterhouses are acquiring cattle reared on illegally cleared land', and these claims are being investigated (Procuradoria da República no Pará, 2016). As several studies have noted, the cattle industry is lagging far behind in adopting effective measures to address Amazon deforestation (Macisaac, 2017).

The fact that the gang is unable to get legal title to the land doesn't seem to cause serious problems either, as it doesn't stop them from running their ranch on the property as before. People living in the region commonly agree: 'the owner is the person who clears the land'. Accordingly, the land thieves are viewed as the rightful owners, and they can readily sell the land on the open market and make a large sum into the bargain. In practice, it seems to make little difference whether those who clear a parcel have legal title to it or not.

The body responsible for ensuring that illegally appropriated public land is returned to state ownership is the federal government's Terra Legal Programme. But people to whom we made inquiries in Pará say that that these officials are doing nothing to reclaim illegally cleared land. We asked the person in charge of the Terra Legal Programme in the west of Pará why measures had not been taken to reclaim the gang's land, but he didn't reply.

All things considered, it seems that Operation Flying Rivers, with its two-year investigation, its 95 federal police, 15 tax experts, 32 IBAMA employees, and 24 arrest warrants, though successful on its own terms, has not been able to put an end to the most serious problem: those deforesting public lands can still keep that land, use it, make hefty profits from it and, in all likelihood, face little punishment. This, to be fair, was something that lay beyond the scope of the federal operation. So Ana Luiza Junqueira Vilela Viacava, her brother, and her husband can go on declaring, at least for now: 'I like land and the security it gives me for the future'.

Time to move on from AJ Vilela's land and drive further north on the BR-163 highway to the town of Novo Progresso, which, we're told, was the stronghold of violent land thieves, whose power is increasing week by week under the Temer government.

References

All web references were checked and still available in June/July 2018 unless otherwise stated.

Cavalcanti, E. (2011) 'A liberação da PCH na Gleba Cristalino pode ter sido troca de favores entre Maggi e o pecuarista Antônio José Junqueira Vilela', *Página do E* [Website] <http://paginadoenock.com.br/a-liberacao-da-pch-na-gleba-cristalino-pode-ter-sido-troca-de-favores-entre-maggi-e-o-pecuarista-antonio-jose-junqueira-vilela-talvez-maggi-saia-limpinho-desta-historia-mas-o-que-nao-pode-mais-deixa/>

CV Nelore Mocho (2016) 'Carlos Viacava está entre as 100 personalidades mais influentes do agronegócio brasileiro', <http://carlosviacava.com.br/NoticiasTexto.aspx?idNoticia=263>

Diário de Cuiabá (2007) 'Episódio da PCH Rochedo é caso à parte', *Diário de Cuiabá* [Website] <http://www.diariodecuiaba.com.br/detalhe.php?cod=278309>

Dinheiro Rural (2011) 'A fórmula secreta da pecuária', [Website] <https://www.dinheirorural.com.br/secao/agronegocios/a-formula-secreta-da-pecuaria>

Gazeta Digital (2007) 'Magistrado manda que empresa pare construção de hidrelétrica', *Gazeta Digital* <http://www.gazetadigital.com.br/

conteudo/show/secao/9/og/1/materia/158064/t/magistrado-manda-que-empresa-pare-construcao-de-hidreletrica>

Glamurama (2013) 'Glamurettes fervem até altas horas na festa de AJ JunqueiraVilela. Confira', *Glamurama* <https://glamurama.uol.com.br/uma-turma-animada-de-glamurettes-ferveu-ate-altas-horas-na-festa-de-aj-junqueira-vilela/>

Jornal Nacional (2016) 'Ministério Público quer manter preso o maior desmatador da Amazônia', *Jornal Nacional* <http://g1.globo.com/jornal-nacional/noticia/2016/10/ministerio-publico-quer-manter-preso-o-maior-desmatador-da-amazonia.html>

Macisaac, T. (2017) 'Cattle industry lags behind in addressing impact on deforestation', *Mongabay* [online] <https://news.mongabay.com/2017/03/cattle-industry-lags-behind-in-addressing-impact-on-deforestation/>

MF Rural (2012) 'MF entrevista Antônio José Junqueira Vilela (AJJ)', [online] <https://www.youtube.com/watch?v=ax_ar9xjEWQ>

Milanez, F. (2010) 'Genocídio na selva', *Vice* [online] <https://www.vice.com/pt_br/article/ezgdwa/genocidio-na-selva-v2n5>

Milanez, F. (2016) 'A morte de Konibu e o crime de genocídio de Romero Jucá', *Carta Capital* [website] <https://www.cartacapital.com.br/sociedade/a-morte-de-konibu-e-o-crime-de-genocidio-de-romero-juca>

Ondei, V. (no date) 'As damas do agronegócio', *Revista Dinheiro Rural* [online] <http://www.canaonline.com.br/mulher/conteudo/as-damas-do-agronegocio.html>

Procuradoria da República no Pará, Rios Voadores: MPF questiona JBS e familia Maggi sobre negocios com os maiores desmatadores da Amazônia <http://www.mpf.mp.br/pa/sala-de-imprensa/noticias-pa/rios-voadores-mpf-questiona-jbs-e-familia-maggi-sobre-negocios-com-os-maiores-desmatadores-da-amazonia>

Racy, S. (2016) 'Sai hoje', Blog Direto da Fonte, *Estadão* [blog] <http://cultura.estadao.com.br/blogs/direto-da-fonte/sai-hoje/>

Ribeiro, V. (2011) 'CPI deve convocar Blairo Maggi a prestar depoimento', *Turma do Epa* [online] <http://www.turmadoepa.com.br/conteudo/show/secao/1/materia/319>

Teodoro, E. (no date) 'Megaempresário falsifica documentação de área de PCHs', *Mato Grosso Notícias* [website] <http://matogrossonoticias.com.br/meio-ambiente/megaempresario-falsifica-documentacao-de-area-de-pch-s/17610>

Torres, M., Doblas, J. and Alarcon, D.F. (2017) 'Dono é quem desmata: conexões entre grilagem e desmatamento no sudoeste paraense', São Paulo: Urutu-branco; Altamira: Instituto Agronômico da Amazônia 2017 <https://www.socioambiental.org/pt-br/noticias-socioambientais/dono-e-quem-desmata>

CHAPTER 11

Land speculators poised to gain control

Land grabbers in Novo Progresso, a frontier town in Pará, built beside the BR-163 highway, are anxious to reap all the benefits of the current boom in land prices. They have long used violence to grab land by illegally evicting peasant families, but now they want to get their hands on protected land in conservation units. This requires a change in legislation, which they are well on the way to achieving, now that their ally, the rural caucus, is so strong in congress and is extracting major concessions from the Temer government.

Novo Progresso is a frontier town in north-west Pará state. 'Here we don't have robberies', a cabby told us proudly on arrival. 'Here everyone is armed'. The weapons are often concealed but, indeed, most locals carry guns, a reality indicative of the region's long history of violence and lawlessness.

Founded in 1991, Novo Progresso sprang up around a clandestine landing strip built to provide a rapid way in and out of this remote, inaccessible region for those earning money – and often a lot of it – through illegal gold mining and logging. Peasant families were arriving too, though travelling more slowly along the unpaved BR-163 highway. The BR-163 is Novo Progresso's main street, and, at the peak of the soya harvest, hundreds of huge lorries rumble through town, stirring up choking clouds of dust. But some residents are happy at the noise and pollution, claiming that it signals progress for the once isolated region. After a wait of almost 45 years, the road's paving is nearly complete, and much of Mato Grosso's bumper soya crop is now flowing along the new northern lorry-and-boat route to the Atlantic coast via the Amazon river, instead of being driven thousands of miles south to the ports of Santos and Paranaguá.

Today, commerce is bustling here, though some hotel and supermarket owners are on bail, awaiting trial for illegal logging, land theft, and conspiracy to commit crimes – all swept up in 2014's Operation Castanheira, a federal bust named after Ezequiel Castanha, owner of the Castanha supermarket chain, who, it was discovered, had earned much more money from his illegal activities than his legal ones (MPF/PA, 2016). But there are few signs that land thieving is

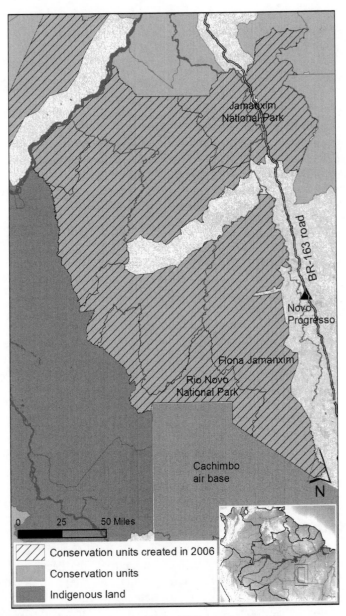

Map 11.1 Conservation units created in 2006 near the BR-163.
Map by Maurício Torres
Source: ISA/Prodes-Inpe

being curbed by the federal operations. When we visited in November 2016, pressure by Novo Progresso land speculators – working with Brazil's agribusiness lobby in the Temer administration and the National Congress – had begun to dismantle Brazil's vast network of conservation units, exposing millions of hectares of currently protected Amazon rainforest to the twin onslaught of deforestation and development. Indeed, the hot topic under discussion was whether or not the Jamanxim National Forest, known as *Flona Jamanxin*, was going to be dismembered.

This conservation unit, covering 1.3 million hectares, an area the size of Puerto Rico, extends alongside the BR-163 to the west of Novo Progresso. It was created, along with seven other conservation units, in 2006 as part of an innovative set of environmental protection measures called the Sustainable BR-163 Plan, drawn up in 2003 when the paving of the highway was announced (MMA, n.d.).

Once a national forest is established, land within it cannot be registered in the name of a private individual. As a result, an Amazon land thief can't occupy a plot, clear it, ranch on it, and then sell it at a great profit. So speculative deforestation – which occurs whenever a new road penetrates Brazilian forest – drops drastically when this kind of conservation unit is established on either side of it, even though the units often exist more on paper than in reality.

However, when *Flona Jamanxim* was created, there were already a few peasant families living inside the unit, and they were understandably reluctant to leave. That fact gave wealthy Novo Progresso land speculators a pretext for rejecting the *Flona*, and they whipped up wide support for their position. The speculators, already active in the region, had expected a land boom with the paving of BR-163 like the ones that had accompanied other new roads. They weren't going to accept a government ban that would prevent them from making a fortune by invading, clearing, and selling off land at a vast profit. They organised protests, blockaded the highway, and published blogs in which they claimed that the *Flona* had 'frozen the region and stopped farmers producing'. They demanded that the conservation unit be abolished or reduced in size.

This political pressure led to a re-evaluation by the federal Chico Mendes Institute for the Conservation of Biodiversity (ICMBio, Instituto Chico Mendes de Conservação da Biodiversidade), the body that administers federal conservation units. The agency's 2009 study assessed the speculators' demand to shrink the *Flona*, and found, contrary to what the latter alleged, that 67 per cent of the land holdings within the unit had been established after it was created in 2006, and that 60 per cent of the new residents didn't live on their plots (ICMBio, 2009). In other words, wealthy land grabbers had been hard at work to seize, deforest, and develop public land.

ICMBio's conclusion: a *Flona* reduction 'would lead to a serious setback in the government's conservation strategy that would have unpredictable consequences, not just for the area of the *Flona* itself, but also for various other conservation units in Amazonia, which would inevitably suffer from pressure from landowners, invasions, and political interests'. The report did, however, recommend that small adjustments be made to satisfy the land claims of peasant families living there before 2006. It recommended that an area of 35,000 hectares – 3.7 per cent of the total – be removed from the *Flona* for them.

This wasn't what the speculators wanted and they went on pressuring the government while continuing to occupy large areas of the *Flona* illegally. IBAMA and ICMBio pushed back and tried to regain control of the unit. In 2008 and 2009, they undertook large-scale enforcement operations, even confiscating cattle reared within the *Flona*. As a result, forest cutting within the unit declined markedly in 2010, 2011, and 2012. But in 2013, ICMBio suffered huge budget cuts, with newspapers describing the institute's situation as penury (Bragança, 2013). It was forced to give up much of its fieldwork, and land thieves and loggers returned to business as usual. *Flona Jamanxim* figured near the top of the list of the country's conservation units in which the most serious illegal forest clearing was taking place (Girardi, 2017).

IBAMA and ICMBio continued running one-off operations, but they couldn't stop the rising tide of land crime. The Institute of Man and the Environment in Amazonia (IMAZON, Instituto do Homem e Meio Ambiente de Amazônia), a research institute, showed that by 2016 the average size of a private holding in the *Flona* had jumped to 1,843 hectares, far more land than any peasant family would occupy (Amazonia Notícia e Informação, 2017). There were many violent conflicts. For instance, in June 2016, when an IBAMA team went to the *Flona* to battle illegal logging, a military policeman was killed. Jair Shmitt, the general co-ordinator of environmental monitoring at IBAMA, described *Flona Jamanxim* as 'one of the most violent conservation units in Amazonia', located in a region which had 'professional assassins involved in illegal felling and in the theft of public land' (Bragança, 2016).

The dismemberment of *Flona Jamanxim*

The impeachment of President Dilma Rousseff in August 2016 and the assumption of government by the agribusiness-friendly Temer administration emboldened the Novo Progresso speculators. They met regularly in Novo Progresso and organised trips to Brasília to talk with the *Bancada Ruralista*, the agribusiness lobby (Folha do Progreso, 2015).

We met Agamenon da Silva Menezes, the president of the Rural Trade Union of Novo Progresso and the spokesman for the landowners, in his office in the centre of town, just after he had returned from one of those Brasília trips. In good spirits, despite his long, tiring bus journey, he told us that the problem with *Flona Jamanxim* was the way it was originally set up: 'This *Flona* was created at full speed; they ordered it to be signed, without following the proper norms'. At the time, there were families living there, he said, and this had been ignored. Smiling, he assured us that everything was going to be sorted out soon, now that there was a more positive atmosphere in Brasília. He was also keen to tell us his views about the environment: 'Brazil is poor because

Photo 11.1 Agamenon da Silva Menezes in front of the trade union building in Novo Progresso.
Photo by Thais Borges

it doesn't deforest. The word 'deforest' is a provocation. In fact, what is happening is an alteration in the forest. The deforested area isn't left bare. It's used for crops, for pasture, for something. A planted forest replaces an unplanted forest'.

Not everyone in Novo Progresso agrees with Agamenon: we met Lincoln Brasil Queiroz in his small garden with lovely tropical flowers – a shady oasis in the hot, grey town. He's one of the few farmers in the region to have legitimate land titles, because his father purchased property from the federal government's land reform institute, INCRA, in the 1970s. He was worried about the political consequences of the possible dismembering of the *Flona*: 'If the land thieves win, those who have organised the campaign will be strengthened', he said. It will send out a harmful message: 'Those who have carried on felling forest, illegally occupying the land, will be rewarded. For the local society, it will seem that crime pays'. The MPF shares his concerns. With rumours circulating about the *Flona's* imminent size reduction, the MPF filed a suit calling for the dismemberment process to be halted and for an intensification in the monitoring of the *Flona* (MPF, n.d.). It also demanded that the region's slaughterhouses be held to account for processing cattle reared on illegally cleared public land.

Agamenon was unruffled by the MPF's actions, probably because he knew what was about to happen. His group, which dictates the editorial line of Novo Progresso's newspaper, *O Progresso*, was supremely confident that they would manage to dismember the conservation units: 'With this, we expect the west region of the state to have much greater economic development with the arrival of heavy investment, both from the private and public sectors' (Ribeiro, 2016). In December 2016, President Temer, with the support of Minister of the Environment José Sarney Filho, signed interim measures MP 756 and MP 758. In the technical note that accompanied the measures, the Ministry of the Environment referred to: 'the great disparity between the proposals presented by the ICMBio and the Association of Producers'. The conflict between the two groups, it said, had made it impossible to manage the *Flona* effectively.

The solution found by the ministry was to rearrange the conservation units. It proposed to remove about half, 743,000 hectares, from the Flona Jamanxim and to give more than half of this land, 438,000 hectares, to the neighbouring national park of Rio Novo, a category with tougher environmental protection. However, the remaining

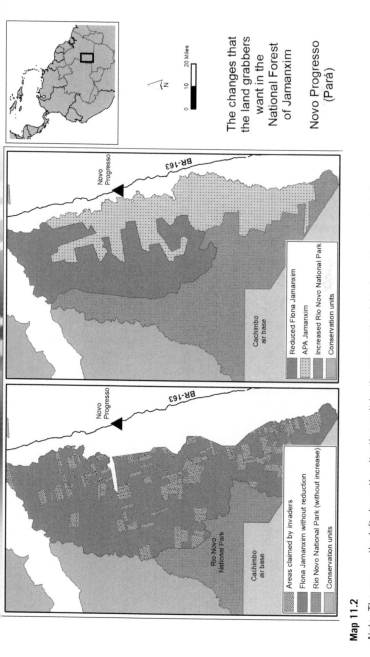

The changes that the land grabbers want in the National Forest of Jamanxim

Novo Progresso (Pará)

Map 11.2

Note: The map on the left shows the situation as it is; the map on the right shows the proposed changes.
Map by Maurício Torres.
Data source: Instituto Brasileiro do Meio Ambiente (IBAMA)

305,000 hectares were to be reclassified as an Area of Environmental Protection: the APA Jamanxim – a much freer conservation classification, which allows land speculators easy access. At the same time, the ministry proposed to remove a relatively small area of 862 hectares from the Jamanxim National Park 'to permit the passage of *Ferrogrão* [Grainrail]', the new commodities railway fast-tracked for construction by President Temer to transport soya and other crops to the north for export.

The measures created a furious reaction, at home and abroad, and President Temer, on a visit to Oslo, suspended them (Gonzales, 2017). The only area that was excluded from the suspension was the 862 hectares required for *Ferrogrão*. It was a triumph for environmentalists, but one that may be temporary. Just a few days later, José Sarney Filho, the environment minister, presented a bill to congress in which the measures to reduce *Flona Jamanxim* were introduced once again, through a bill rather than by presidential decree. In early 2018, the bill was still making its way through congress.

Taking the federal axe to Sustainable BR-163

If the bill is passed, which is probable, the dismembering of the *Flona Jamanxim* will sound the death knell for the Sustainable BR-163 Plan, designed 15 years ago to demonstrate that the paving of roads and forest protection can be compatible in the Amazon. In truth, the whittling away began much earlier. According to Brent Millikan, Amazon Programme Director at the NGO International Rivers, the Sustainable BR-163 Plan of 2006 was soon superseded by the Programme for the Acceleration of Growth (PAC) of 2007, a high-profile government programme for heavy investment in infrastructure. At that time, the overriding priority of the Workers' Party (PT) was to stay in power, he said, and, to achieve this, they 'formed alliances with traditional political and economic groups who were interested, above all, in getting their hands on public assets – public money, natural resources, and so on – and this was absolutely incompatible with the objectives of the Sustainable BR-163 Plan'.

Even before the planned dismemberment of the *Flona*, the Plan had clearly failed. According to Juan Doblas, who monitors the region's deforestation for the Geoprocessing Laboratory at the NGO Instituto Socioambiental (ISA), '10 years after the licensing of the work, accumulated deforestation had reached the worst projections' made about the impact of the paving of the road on the forest. According to Doblas, 'the situation would have been much worse had it not been for the creation of the conservation units', but now even this gain may be reversed.

It was President Dilma Rousseff who found a way around the long, complex procedure in congress that had previously been required to reduce the size of protected areas. She bypassed all this by using *Medidas Provisórias* (MPs), interim measures, which can be decreed by the president without congressional approval (Camargo and Torres, 2016). She did so out of her desire to build the large São Luiz do Tapajós hydroelectric project, and, in 2012, exercised her executive power to redraw the borders of conservation units that stood in the way of this mega-dam. Although the construction of the São Luiz do Tapajós dam has been halted, thanks in large part to mobilisation by indigenous groups, the precedent of using MPs to alter the limits of protected areas was established and is now providing Temer with cover for his attempt to dismember *Flona Jamanxim*. These boundary shifts provide crystal clear examples of how conservation is made subordinate to the government's current infrastructure and agribusiness expansion plans.

ICMBio Director for the Creation and Management of Conservation Units Paul Carneiro admitted that, if it happens, the dismembering will harm *Flona Jamanxim*, but said 'we were witnessing such an escalation in the conflict [between the ICMBio and the land grabbers] that all possibility of dialogue was being destroyed' (Maisonnave, 2016). But another ICMBio employee, speaking off the record, is horrified at the precedent that will be established. 'The reduction in the size of *Flona Jamanxim* will show criminals that, if they invade and clear a conservation unit, they can get it reclassified and keep the land', he told us. 'I want to know if Brasília will come in the future and help us contain the invasion of more conservation units, as this is sure to happen'. Doblas agrees. He said that ICMBio has surrendered to the bullying tactics of the land thieves: 'When the government declares an APA on the frontier of the expansion of agribusiness, it is effectively reinforcing a speculative race in which various agents are going to fight over the land, which is now seen as "thievable", and then clear it and occupy it'.

Now that they sense they are on the verge of victory, the land speculators seem hungry for more. Other conservation units are being targeted: in January 2017, the government announced a plan to radically reduce the size of conservation units in the state of

Amazonas – dismembering the biological reserve of Manicoré, national park of Acari, and national forests of Aripuanã and Urupadi, and extinguishing the APA of the Campos de Manicoré. If that plan goes ahead, about one million hectares will lose the environmental protection they currently enjoy. In February 2017, an open letter from 21 conservation NGOs called on the Brazilian government to rethink the proposal (Amazonia, 2017).

But, based on the political strength, influence, and reach of the agribusiness lobby, a change in policy seems unlikely. In fact, Eliseu Padilha, who heads the general staff of the Presidency of the Republic, has himself been accused of land theft in another conservation unit, the Serra Ricardo Franco Park in Mato Grosso. Adriana Ramos, co-ordinator of policy and law at the ISA, told us that 'agribusiness's strategy, as expressed by the Parliamentary Front for Agriculture and Livestock, is to weaken and neutralise the scope of environmental legislation and the territorial rights of traditional people and communities'. What we are witnessing, she says, is 'an attack on social and environmental rights by agribusiness'.

Not surprisingly, the landowners see it differently. In his interview with us, Agamenon da Silva Menezes said that society has always progressed and that change is inevitable. Leaning towards us, he asked: 'Do you miss dinosaurs?'

References

All web references were checked and still available in June/July 2018 unless otherwise stated.

Amazônia Notícia e Informação (2017) 'Nota de repúdio a proposta de redução de UCs no Amazonas', *Amazônia Notícia e Informação* [website] <http://amazonia.org.br/2017/02/nota-de-repudio-a-proposta-de-reducao-de-ucs-no-amazonas/>

Amazônia Notícia e Informação (2017) 'Reduzir unidades de conservação aumenta o desmatamento e incentiva a grilagem: o exemplo da Flona do Jamanxim', *Amazônia Notícia e Informação* [online] <http://amazonia.org.br/2017/03/reduzir-unidades-de-conservacao-aumenta-o-desmatamento-e-incentiva-a-grilagem-o-exemplo-da-flona-do-jamanxim/>

Bragança, D. (2013) 'Segundo corte no orçamento pode levar ICMBio à penúria', *O Eco* [online] <http://www.oeco.org.br/reportagens/27551-segundo-corte-no-orcamento-pode-levar-icmbio-a-penuria/>

Bragança, D. (2016) 'Floresta Nacional do Jamanxim: policial é morto durante operação do Ibama', *O Eco* [website] <http://www.oeco.

org.br/noticias/floresta-nacional-do-jamanxim-policial-e-morto-durante-operacao-do-ibama/>

Camargo, M.L. and Torres M. (2016) 'Redução na medida: a Medida Provisória Nº 558/2012 e a arbitrariedade da desafetação de unidades de conservação na Amazônia', in D.F. Alarcon, B. Millikan, and M. Torres (eds), *Ocekadi: hydroelectric dams, socio-environmental conflicts, and resistance in the Tapajós basin*, International Rivers Brasil and Federal University of Western Para [online] <https://www.internationalrivers.org/resources/ocekadi-hydroelectric-dams-socio-environmental-conflicts-and-resistance-in-the-tapaj%C3%B3s>

Folha do Progresso (2015) 'Delimitação da Flona Jamanxim, cada dia mais difícil', [online] <http://www.folhadoprogresso.com.br/delimitacao-da-flona-jamanximcada-dia-mais-dificil/>

Girardi, G. (2017) 'Desmatamento cresce em unidades de conservação da Amazônia', 18 March 2017 <http://sustentabilidade.estadao.com.br/noticias/geral,desmatamento-cresce-em-unidades-de-conservacao-no-meio-da-amazonia,70001704735>

Gonzales, J. (2017) 'Norway vexed as Brazil sends mixed message on Amazon forest protection', *Mongabay* [online] <https://news.mongabay.com/2017/06/norway-vexed-as-brazil-sends-mixed-message-on-amazon-forest-protection/>

ICMBio (2009) 'Estudo técnico de revisão dos limites da Floresta Nacional do Jamanxim', *Instituto Chico Mendes de Conservação da Biodiversidade* [website] <https://documentacao.socioambiental.org/noticias/anexo_noticia/11685_20100503_170047.pdf>

Maisonnave, F. (2016) 'Temer flexibiliza preservacão em floresta do Pará e legaliza posseiros', *Folha de S.Paulo* [online] <http://www1.folha.uol.com.br/ambiente/2016/12/1843269-medida-provisoria-reduz-nivel-de-protecao-legal-de-floresta-no-para.shtml>

MMA (no date) 'Projeto BR-163', *Ministério do Meio Ambiente* [online] <http://www.mma.gov.br/florestas/projeto-br-163>

MPF/PA (2016) 'MPF/PA: Justiça determina nova prisão de desmatador pego pela operação Castanheira', *Ministério Público Federal* [online] <http://www.mpf.mp.br/pa/sala-de-imprensa/noticias-pa/justica-determina-nova-prisao-de-desmatador-pego-pela-operacao-castanheira>

MPF (no date) 'Ação do MPF pela não redução da Flona do Jamanxim sem estudos e consulta pública', *Ministério Público Federal* <http://www.mpf.mp.br/pa/sala-de-imprensa/documentos/10/11/2016/acao-do-mpf-pela-nao-reducao-da-flona-do-jamanxim-sem-estudos-e-consulta-publica/view>

Ribeiro, E. (2016) 'Flona do Jamanxim', *Progresso Noticia* [online] <http://progressonoticia.blogspot.com.br/2016/12/flona-do-jamanxim.html>

CHAPTER 12
The guardians of the forest

The Kayapó Indians have opened an office in the town of Novo Progresso, the land grabbers' heartland on the BR-163 highway. The indigenous groups are Brazil's best land stewards. Yet their land rights have been threatened, first by the Dilma Rousseff administration and, far more aggressively, by Michel Temer's government. With the support of social movements and NGOs, the indigenous groups are fighting back, with considerable success.

While Novo Progresso is the land grabbers heartland, it is also home to an office of the leaders of the indigenous people who are arguably the forest's best guardians and protectors. There we met indigenous leader Anhë Kayapó. 'As president of the Kabu Institute', he told us, 'I keep an eye on everyone coming into our forest – gold miners, loggers, land thieves (who do most of the deforestation), and so on. We protect our entire area so it will remain as it always was'. He spoke briefly to us about the long indigenous occupation of the land and the Indians' mistrust of those he calls 'whites'. He then added brusquely: 'That's all I have to tell you', ending the interview. He shook our hands firmly and left us alone in the room.

Anhë Kayapó is the leader of the Kayapó Mekrãgnoti, who live in the indigenous territory of Baú, which lies to the east of the BR-163. Unlike the Munduruku Indians we visited earlier in our trip – highly democratic and famous for long meetings aimed at reaching consensus – the Kayapó are more hierarchical and dislike drawn-out discussions. They prefer action to debate, so the brevity of our meeting didn't surprise us.

Anhë Kayapó's distrust of 'whites' is also understandable in light of the near perpetual state of conflict that marks the history of indigenous land claims and white settlement in the Amazon – a contentious relationship that seems about to boil over as Brazil's agribusiness-backed Temer administration pushes ahead with anti-indigenous policies.

The Baú territory, inhabited and protected by the Kayapó Mekrãgnoti and other indigenous groups, covers 1.5 million hectares. When combined with surrounding indigenous territories and conservation units, the land conserved in this region totals a staggering

Photo 12.1 Anhë Kayapó, president of the Kabu Institute and leader of the Kayapó Mekrãgnoti, Indians who live in the indigenous territory of Baú.
Photo by Thais Borges

28 million hectares – one of the largest protected wild corridors in the world, and a vast swathe vital to conserving Amazon tropical rainforest.

The Kayapó aren't the only Indians in Brazil to resolutely defend their forest territory against intruders. In fact, the Amazon's indigenous people do a better job curbing deforestation than any other group of land managers. According to data for 2014 from the Forest Transparency Bulletin of Amazônia Legal, 59 per cent of that year's illegal deforestation took place on privately held land, 27 per cent occurred within conservation units, and 13 per cent within agrarian reform settlements. But just 1 per cent of deforestation took place on indigenous lands (FUNAI, 2014).

As a result, Brazil's nearly 900,000 Indians, belonging to 305 peoples and speaking 274 languages, not only make a major contribution to the country's social and cultural diversity, but they have proven to be unparalleled stewards of ecological diversity as well (*Jornal Nacional*, 2012). But land grabbers, with unprecedented political support from the government, have spotted an opportunity to gain access to long-coveted indigenous land. Their allies in congress, the *Bancada Ruralista*, are pushing through changes in the legislation to weaken indigenous rights, and in their home states in the Amazon basin they are invading indigenous reserves.

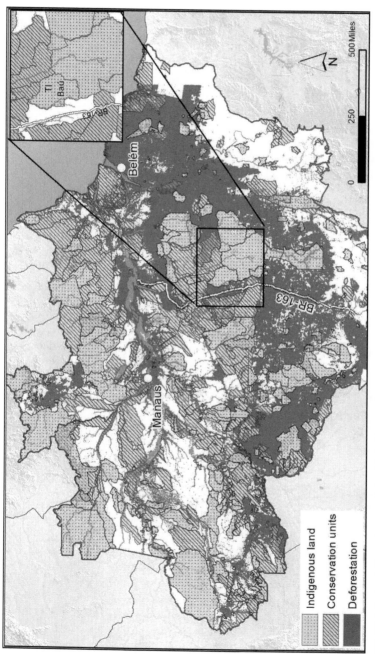

Map 12.1 Deforestation gains pace but not in indigenous land.
Map by Maurício Torres

But the Indians are fighting back, with Brazil's 1988 constitution, agreed after the end of the military dictatorship, providing a strong legal basis for their struggle. Until then, indigenous land had been ceded to Indians only provisionally, until they were assimilated into so-called national society. Among other advances, the new constitution brought Indians the right to be Indians forever. It was a turning point for indigenous people in a century that, until then, had been characterised by massacres. During the 25 years of the military dictatorship alone, it is estimated that at least 8,300 Indians were assassinated (Amazônia Real, 2014). One key advance under the new constitution was its recognition of the Indians' right to the permanent possession of their land. But working out exactly which land was theirs and disentangling competing claims proved to be a complex, slow business, with the official demarcation of indigenous boundaries still dragging on almost 30 years after the new constitution became law.

Now that process – far from complete – has been halted by the Temer administration and Brazil's congress, which are openly hostile to the idea of recognising more indigenous land. This, of course, has major repercussions for Indians whose land claims have yet to be settled. It means, for example, that there is virtually no chance at the moment of ending what a mission of the European Parliament has called 'the genocide of the Guarani Kaiowá people' (CDHM, 2016). Every time the Indians try to reoccupy their traditional land, they face threats from private militias employed by agribusiness. The Guarani Kaiowá have been tortured and assassinated, and suffer from high rates of malnutrition, alcoholism, and suicide.

Failed by the PT

Like social movements throughout Brazil, indigenous people placed high hopes in President Luiz Inácio Lula da Silva, who, in 2002, became the first person from a working-class family to be elected to the country's highest office, as the candidate of the Workers' Party (PT). But Lula did not live up to these expectations. His social policies, widely praised for tackling the country's historic problem of profound inequality, were directed mainly to the poor living on the margins of large cities. The difficulties faced by indigenous and traditional communities were never a priority for Lula.

The leader Gersem Baniwa, from the Baniwa ethnic group in the state of Amazonas, summarized well what many Indians felt at the time:

> After two decades of intense struggle by the Brazilian indigenous movement and a historic political conquest by the Workers' Party and Lula ... it would be a pleasure to be able to talk about the historical gains ... made in the field of indigenous peoples' rights. But, unfortunately, this is not the feeling that prevails among indigenous peoples. Instead, they feel disappointment and doubts. Their state of mind is not worse because, thanks to recent advances, indigenous people no longer put their hope in a party or a saviour of the country but in their own strength and capacity for resistance, mobilisation, and struggle (Baniwa, n.d.).

Lula's two presidential terms saw only 81 new indigenous territories recognised – a significant drop compared with the 118 designated during the two terms of his predecessor, Fernando Henrique Cardoso (known as FHC), a president whom the Indians had never regarded as an ally (Povos Indígenas do Brasil, 2017). In part, the slower progress under Lula was understandable, as FHC had dealt with the least controversial indigenous territory designations, leaving his successor to handle

Photo 12.2 Munduruku woman and child.
Photo by Maurício Torres

the more complex and problematic cases, which often involved serious conflicts.

Under President Dilma Rousseff, who took office in 2011, government relations with indigenous peoples only worsened. 'There was a real rupture in indigenous policy from the Lula to the Dilma governments', said Márcio Santilli, a founding member of the ISA and a former president of the government's indigenous agency, FUNAI. During Dilma's time in office, only 26 indigenous territories were created, a poor showing that would have been even worse if she hadn't rapidly signed decrees establishing reserves during the final days of her government, when she knew her impeachment was imminent.

Dilma's indigenous-unfriendly policies were the result of 'the radical expression of an almost desperate strategy to promote economic growth at any price', Santilli explained. 'As well as reducing dramatically the rate at which indigenous territories were established, her government mostly appointed temporary presidents of FUNAI, and cut the agency's budget. [Dilma] also reduced the rate at which land titles were given to *quilombolas* [areas occupied by runaway slaves] and at which conservation units and agrarian reform settlements were created'. All this showed, Santilli concluded, that her government was reluctant to conserve land for social and environmental purposes, and instead supported largely unregulated economic development in Amazonia.

Dilma's main vehicle for unleashing economic progress was her Programme for the Acceleration of Growth (PAC), an ambitious government programme first announced by Lula, then greatly expanded during her government. PAC led to huge investments in highways, energy, and water resource projects – all with a view to increasing exports and promoting economic growth. Cleber César Buzatto, executive director of the Missionary Indigenous Council (CIMI, Conselho Misionário do Índio), an important Catholic institution that has been working with Brazilian Indians since 1972, said that Dilma subordinated the rights of indigenous peoples to the demands of the PAC: 'A prime example of this was the construction of the Belo Monte hydroelectric power plant on the Xingu river in the state of Pará', he said.

The indigenous impacts of the Belo Monte hydroelectric dam – one of the largest in the world – were so severe that, in 2015, Thais Santi, the prosecutor for the MPF in Altamira, told us: 'There is a process of ethnic extermination under way in Belo Monte by which the federal government continues with the old colonial practice of integrating the Indians into the hegemonic society'. The MPF is currently suing the Brazilian federal government and construction company Norte Energia for the crime of ethnocide against Xingu river indigenous communities (Mongabay, 2015).

Failed by FUNAI

The anthropologist Márcio Meira was president of FUNAI from 2007 to 2012, when the agency adopted a raft of policies that enraged indigenous groups. These included agreeing to the licensing of Belo Monte and other hydroelectric dams, such as the Teles Pires and São Manoel projects in the Tapajós river basin, along with a controversial restructuring of FUNAI itself. Meira said later that he was aware at the time of the emergence of formidable new anti-indigenous forces: 'When I was president of FUNAI, it was clear to me that an anti-indigenous wave was gathering force in Brazilian society, mainly due to the power of the heirs of the old agrarian elites, who were launching an attack on land in the north and north-west of the country' (Milanez, 2013).

According to Meira, seismic shifts in the national economy fuelled hostility to indigenous land claims: 'There has been a decline in manufacturing output, while agricultural production and agricultural exports have increased', he explained. 'The Brazilian economy has become increasingly dependent on agribusiness, and this has had political repercussions. It is not a question of people being against the Indians because they are Indians or even because they have too much land. The problem is that the Indians have lands these political actors want'.

The *Bancada Ruralista* has long cast hungry eyes over indigenous reserves and other conserved Amazon lands. Under Dilma, the lobby's power and influence grew. In a June 2013 press release, National Congress Senator Kátia Abreu claimed that activists had seized control of FUNAI and were causing trouble: 'Ideological militants inside FUNAI, linked to CIMI and national and foreign NGOs, are encouraging the Indians to invade productive lands', she claimed. Abreu, also president of the Confederation of Agriculture and Livestock (CNA, Confederação da Agricultura e Pecuária) and later to be Dilma's agriculture minister, went on to say: 'The CNA supports the idea of adopting a new indigenous policy, in which decisions are taken not only by FUNAI, but with the participation of other ministries and federal government bodies. It is unacceptable that a question as important as [indigenous territory designation] is in the hands of a single body, staffed by ideological militants who are not furthering the national interest'. Now this proposal has become reality.

Targeted by the Temer government

Michel Temer received crucial support from the *Bancada Ruralista* in his controversial bid for power, which succeeded provisionally in April 2016 and became permanent four months later. From the beginning, he made it clear that, as president, he would reverse the indigenous land measures that the justice minister and FUNAI president had rushed through during the last months of Dilma's administration (Iglesias and Mariz, 2016). He also promised the *Bancada Ruralista* that he would roll back indigenous rights. But, with indigenous groups and their supporters intent on damage control, Temer hasn't yet achieved all his goals.

At the end of 2016, with the government reeling from corruption accusations, it still found time to issue new draft regulations changing the administrative procedure for marking out indigenous land. Indians and NGOs linked to the indigenous movement reacted angrily, calling the plan an unprecedented aberration that would make it impossible for the state to carry out its constitutional obligation to recognise indigenous ownership over its land (ISA, 2016). The reaction was so strong that the proposal had to be withdrawn. But, on 18 January 2017, the justice ministry issued Ministerial Order 68, another attempt to push through the same changes. Once again, the reaction was fierce and, just a few hours after Temer openly supported the new order, it was revoked (Borges, 2017).

But that wasn't the end. Soon after, the justice ministry published Ministerial Order 80, a watered-down version of the earlier proposal. Even so, it contained an important change in the way indigenous lands are recognised, creating a specialised technical group to do the job (Gonzales, 2017). Prior to Ministerial Order 80, indigenous lands were recognised and borders established through a technical process carried out by experts, including anthropologists, within FUNAI. But Order 80 brings new bodies into the decision-making process, including some known to be hostile to the Indians, along with professionals with no specialist indigenous knowledge. This is close to what Senator Kátia Abreu was calling for in 2013. According to Juliana de Paula Batista, an ISA lawyer, the government's intention was to 'interfere politically in technical studies' (Klein, 2017).

Indigenous groups began to worry that Temer had more draconian plans. Federal Deputy Osmar Serraglio, a hard-line politician, had long campaigned for curtailment of the constitutional rights of Indians, traditional communities, and *quilombolas*. He repeatedly said that no more land should be given to Indians, because 'land doesn't fill stomachs' (Leite, 2017). In other words, Indians are a welfare problem, which should be resolved through federal hand-outs of food; they shouldn't be entrusted with land. In February 2017, Temer put Serraglio at the head of the justice ministry, which oversees FUNAI. From the indigenous perspective, the fox now ran the hen house. Serraglio didn't last long in office, being sacked in May 2017. But anti-indigenous sentiment remained strong.

The government offensive to limit indigenous rights is gaining momentum. In March 2017, Temer restructured FUNAI, abolishing 87 of the 770 primary managerial positions in the agency, and creating new barriers to the appointment of replacements. The personnel most affected by these cuts dealt with the demarcation of indigenous land and the provision of environmental licences for infrastructure projects such as dams. Antônio Fernandes Toninho Costa, FUNAI president at the time, was not consulted in the restructuring (De Souza, 2017). Márcio Santilli was outraged: 'The government and congress are rotten and the rights of the whole population, including Indians and

Photo 12.3 Federal Deputy Osmar Serraglio.
Photo by Chamber of Deputies, Brasília

traditional populations, are threatened'. From Santilli's perspective the one bright light is that the indigenous movement is resisting courageously and has not been co-opted by Temer's government.

Indeed, despite recent gains, agribusiness isn't having it all its own way: both the industry and the government have been rocked by recent scandals and plagued by infighting. Not long after Serraglio's appointment as justice minister, for example, a federal police operation, codenamed *Carne Fraca* (Weak Meat), revealed a large-scale criminal scheme in which inspectors and slaughterhouses colluded to circumvent the country's public health controls. China and other buyers of Brazilian meat banned shipments. Serraglio's name was mentioned in the evidence. JBS, the world's largest meatpacking company, which is one of the companies under investigation, was the leading funder of Serraglio's electoral campaign in 2014 (De olho nos ruralistas, 2017). 'Those behind the anti-indigenous offensive will find growing resistance both from Indians and from other sectors of society', concluded Santilli.

The movement carried out a major show of strength with an event on 24–28 April 2017. The initiative, called the *Acampamento Terra Livre* (Free Land Camp), brought together about 3,000 indigenous leaders from across the nation. They set up camp in Brasília and hosted marches, debates, protests, and cultural events. The indigenous leaders also sought meetings with the executive, legislative, and judicial branches of the government. The aim was 'to unify struggles in defence of the Indian people'. With Brazil still in its worst economic recession ever – the Temer government wracked by scandal and its popularity as low as Dilma's in the month before she was impeached (Temer had a 27 per cent approval rate at the time, which decreased to 23 per cent by the end of September 2017) – the Free Land Camp made a significant impact.

The key role indigenous communities play in Amazon rainforest protection, combined with the significant carbon sequestration those forests provide, means that the outcome of the current land rights battle matters greatly, not just for indigenous groups, or even for Brazil, but for the whole world. It was indicative of the courage and assertiveness of the Kayapó Indians that they had decided to open an office in Novo Progresso, the *Bancada Ruralista's* heartland. But it's time to return to our interview with the leader of the land thieves, with whom we had discussed *Flona Jamanxim* (see Chapter 11).

References

All web references were checked and still available in June/July 2018 unless otherwise stated.

Amazônia Real (2014) 'Comissão da verdade: ao menos 8,3 mil índios foram mortos na ditadura', [online] <http://amazoniareal.com.br/comissao-da-verdade-ao-menos-83-mil-indios-foram-mortos-na-ditadura-militar/>

Baniwa, G. (no date) 'Expectativas do movimento indígena no cenário atual' [website] <http://www.abant.org.br/conteudo/005COMISSOESGTS/Documentos%20da%20CAI/Expectativas.doc>

Borges, A. (2017) 'Governo muda regras de demarcação de terras indígenas', *O Estado de S. Paulo* 18 January 2017 <https://politica.estadao.com.br/noticias/geral,governo-muda-regra-de-demarcacao-para-terras-indigenas,70001633615>

CDHM (2016) 'Genocídio de povo Guarani-Kaiowá é incontestável, conclui missão do Parlamento Europeu e CDHM', *Human rights and minorities commission, Chamber of Deputies* <http://www2.camara.leg.br/atividade-legislativa/comissoes/comissoes-permanentes/cdhm/noticias/genocidio-de-povo-guarani-kaiowa-no-ms-e-incontestavel-conclui-missao-do-parlamento-europeu-e-cdhm>

De Olho nos Ruralistas (2017) '"Carne Fraca": JBS foi maior doadora de campanha de Osmar Serraglio', [website] <https://deolhonosruralistas.com.br/2017/03/17/carne-fraca-jbs-foi-maior-doadora-de-campanha-de-osmar-serraglio-pmdb/>

De Souza, O.B. (2017) 'Temer e Serraglio aprofundam desmonte da Funai', *Notícias Socioambientais* [online] <https://www.socioambiental.org/pt-br/noticias-socioambientais/temer-e-serraglio-aprofundam-desmonte-da-funai?utm_medium=email&utm_source=transactional&utm_campaign=manchetes%40socioambiental.org>

FUNAI (2014) 'Terras indígenas apresentam o menor índice de desmatamento na Amazônia Legal', [website] <http://www.funai.gov.br/index.php/comunicacao/noticias/2914-terras-indigenas-apresentam-o-menor-indice-de-desmatamento-na-amazonia-legal>

Gonzales, J. (2017) 'Brazil alters indigenous land demarcation process, sparking conflict', *Mongabay* [website] <https://news.mongabay.com/2017/02/brazil-alters-indigenous-land-demarcation-process-sparking-conflict/>

Iglesias, S. and Mariz, R. (2016) 'Temer diz a ruralistas que vai revisar desapropriações e demarcações', *O Globo* <https://oglobo.globo.com/brasil/temer-diz-ruralistas-que-vai-revisar-desapropriacoes-demarcacoes-19202640>

ISA (2016) 'Na prática, proposta do governo Temer acaba com demarcações de Terras indígenas', Instituto Socioambiental (ISA) 12 December 2016 <https://www.socioambiental.org/pt-br/blog/blog-do-isa/na-pratica-proposta-do-governo-temer-acaba-com-demarcacoes-de-terras-indigenas>

Jornal Nacional (2012) 'Brasil tem população de quase 900 mil índios, aponta IBGE', *Jornal Nacional* [online] <http://g1.globo.com/jornal-nacional/noticia/2012/08/brasil-tem-populacao-de-quase-900-mil-indios-aponta-ibge.html>

Klein, T. (2017) 'Governo revoga portarias, mas mantém GT para avaliar demarcações', *Notícias Socioambientais* [online] <https://www.socioambiental.org/pt-br/noticias-socioambientais/governo-revoga-portaria-mas-mantem-gt-para-avaliar-demarcacoes>

Leite, M. (2017) 'Atlas revela que latifúndios superam áreas protegidas', *Folha de S. Paulo* [website] <http://www1.folha.uol.com.br/colunas/marceloleite/2017/03/1867657-atlas-revela-que-latifundio-supera-as-areas-protegidas.shtml>

Milanez, F. (2013) 'Uma onda anti-indígena', *ALAI* [website] <https://www.alainet.org/pt/active/67908>

Mongabay (2015) 'Brazilian government charged with ethnocide in building Amazon dam', *Mongabay* [online] <https://news.mongabay.com/2015/12/brazils-government-charged-with-ethnocide-in-building-of-amazon-dam/>

Povos Indígenas do Brasil (2017) 'Demarcação nos últimos sete governos', [website] <https://pib.socioambiental.org/pt/c/0/1/2/demarcacoes-nos-ultimos-governos>

CHAPTER 13
Deforestation becomes big business

Land in the state of Pará increases in value one hundredfold – or even two hundredfold – when it is cleared of forest. Not surprisingly, land grabbers compete among themselves to clear-fell public forest. At times, peasant families, anxious to obtain a small plot of land for themselves, get caught up in this violent tussle. With the backing of their allies in congress, land grabbers openly send armed militias to evict them.

On the Amazon frontier, where many people operate outside the law, you often hear locals speak in code – something journalists learn to listen for. So our ears pricked up as we prepared to film the interview with Agamenon da Silva Menezes, president of the Novo Progresso Rural Farmers' Union in Pará. A man rushed in, speaking urgently to Agamenon without a glance at us: 'They're taking over the area. We need to do something. Right away'. Agamenon raised a hand to silence him and responded calmly: 'OK. Don't worry. We'll talk later'. Then he turned to us and said abruptly: 'Shall we begin?' It was only later, when Agamenon described the activities of his farmers' union during the interview, that the penny dropped: the 'something' the man mentioned was code for an illegal violent act; and the 'they' referred to settlers engaged in a land occupation organised by the Castelo dos Sonhos Rural Workers' Union, at a location known as KM Mil. What the gate-crasher was calling for was the illegal eviction of these settlers by an armed militia.

Coincidentally, we'd come to talk to Agamenon about this landless peasant occupation. The KM Mil settlement was located near the thousand kilometre marker on the BR-163, 1,000 kilometres (620 miles) from Cuiabá, the capital of Mato Grosso. Two days earlier, we had visited the 80 families taking part in the occupation. They were living in rough shacks, with roofs covered in black plastic sheeting to keep out the rain. These shacks resembled hundreds of other temporary lean-tos that have sprung up across Brazil in the last 30 years as part of the occupations organised by Brazil's Landless Workers' Movement (MST, Movimento dos Trabalhadores Rurais Sem Terra) and other social movements trying to force authorities to carry out much-needed agrarian reform.

Photo 13.1 Agamenon da Silva Menezes, president of the Novo Progresso Rural Farmers' Union in Pará state.
Photo by Thais Borges

Photo 13.2 Alenquer, in a flak jacket, talking to settlers at KM Mil.
Photo by Thais Borges

The KM Mil settlement, about 16 kilometers (10 miles) from the highway, was situated at the extreme edge of a large area of cleared forest. Turning their back on the cleared area, the peasants had started the hard work of clearing dense undergrowth and trees. We'd arrived with Aluisio Sampaio, a trade unionist known as Alenquer, the primary leader of the occupation, so the settlers didn't treat us with mistrust but spoke freely. One settler explained why the community was moving into the forest: 'Of course, we'd have liked to have occupied the already cleared area, but it's far too dangerous. It's valuable land. People will fight tooth and nail to keep hold of it. People aren't so interested in the forest'. This may sound like bizarre logic, with deforested land and denuded soil deemed to be worth far more than exuberant, life-packed primary Amazon forest. But this is the way it is on the Amazon frontier, where cleared land, which can be sold to ranchers and farmers, is far more valuable (in dollars) than rainforest. Until it is reversed, this way of thinking and acting will make it impossible to end the rampant forest destruction happening all over the region.

Landless peasants vs land thieves

So the settlers told us they would never think of moving into large deforested areas. To do so would almost assuredly draw violence against them because those who have cleared the forest consider themselves the owners of the land. Instead, these landless Brazilians are continually pushed deeper into the rainforest. It is wealthy land operators who do the pushing. These politically connected land grabbers, backed up by their violent militias, turn large stolen tracts into no-go areas – even when the land claimed and deforested is publicly owned (which it often is) and should not be taken over by private landowners. The state scarcely ever reclaims the land, and the thieves eventually get some kind of title to it, becoming its owners. In other words, on the Amazon frontier, crime pays.

This leaves landless peasants with little choice. If they wish to survive economically, they must clear virgin forest. But even that act often benefits the land thieves: they use their influence to get officials from IBAMA to inspect the modest damage the settlers do to the forest, drawing attention away from the much greater harm the land thieves are causing with their own illegal land grabs. In the end, the big land thieves sometimes get the peasants' land too, kicking them off the plots they've cleared, forcing them deeper into the forest. And so the cycle begins again. Though far from being the main cause of Amazonian deforestation, this dynamic provides a graphic example of how life on the frontier typically works, with the wealthy dominating and exploiting the poor. It is an upside-down world: studies show that, ironically, the only legitimate claimants to Amazon public lands are the peasant families. This is because, in the 1970s and 1980s, large areas of the Amazon, including those currently in dispute, were set aside by the federal government specifically for the purpose of carrying out agrarian reform – but the programme was never properly implemented.

When we arrived at the KM Mil settlement, a woman was cooking lunch for a dozen people, some of whom had been clearing forest. She invited us to join them. While we ate, settler Ivanor da Silva Felizardo told us about his life: 'I left Sinop [further south on the BR-163, see Chapter 5] for lack of prospects. There was no way of getting on. Here everything is more raw; it's possible to make something of your life. My luck was to get 100 hectares [247 acres] through the trade union'.

With the rural workers' trade union organising the landless occupation, the peasants felt they had some legitimacy and protection from violence: 'The union is a legal organisation', Ivanor told us, 'we have been here for about 90 days, and everything has gone well so far'. Even so, tension hung in the air. There were few women or children at the site, and some settlers admitted to often feeling afraid. 'They [the land thieves] want to get rid of me', said leader Alenquer, who wears a flak jacket all the time. 'They make threats against me on television, on radio, in the market, at home. I've got used to it. They don't frighten me. And it won't help them to kill me. We've trained various leaders along the BR-163. If they kill me, someone else will take my place'.

Photo 13.3 Gathering for lunch at KM Mil.
Photo by Thais Borges

After lunch, another settler, who didn't want to give his name, told us how the occupation had come about: a few years earlier, a man he called 'the rightful owner' had been 'forced off the land, by brute force' by a certain Tião, a much-feared gunman from the AJ Vilela gang (see Chapter 10). 'After [Tião] took over, hardly anyone who set foot in here returned alive', he said. There were many murders, the settler told us. But after the arrest of AJ Vilela in 2016 by federal police, the land's 'rightful owner' reappeared. He was keen to regain control of his land, so came to the rural trade union with a proposal: he would give the peasants some land to clear and keep. The peasants were surprised at this act of generosity, but believed 'the rightful owner' was a good man who simply wanted to help them. 'We signed a contract, it's all legalised', the settler told us. 'We are very happy. It's going to work out well'.

However, things were more complicated than first appeared. The settlers learned later that 'the rightful owner' wasn't the only one eyeing this valuable piece of real estate that had become available after the arrest of the gang. And despite calling himself 'the rightful owner', the man behind the deal was, in fact, just another land thief – the first to occupy the land illegally before being driven off by the more powerful and violent AJ Vilela gang. 'The rightful owner' refused to be interviewed, saying that publicity would make it more likely that he would be assassinated, but it seemed to us that he probably planned to use the landless peasants as pawns and as a human shield. He knew the settlers were determined to keep their plots and would defend their camp fiercely. It could be a good deal for the owner: if the peasants drove off the militias hired by other land thieves, then he would get to keep an extremely valuable area of cleared land, while 'giving' the settlers a relatively small piece of forest.

Our interview with Agamenon demonstrated that the settlers would not find it easy to hang on to the land they'd claimed. To him, the peasant families were invaders who had to be evicted, whatever the cost. Though reluctant to talk about KM Mil specifically, Agamenon spoke frankly about how he used militias made up of hired thugs to resolve situations of this nature: 'If they [the settlers] leave on their own accord, fine. If they won't go, we make them. We do what it takes. If they use clubs against us, we use clubs. If they use knives, we use knives. If they use dogs, we use dogs … the way it is done depends on them … but in the end we get them out'.

It was surprising to find that Agamenon was willing to talk so openly on camera about sending in his own militia – utterly illegal in Brazil. But since the fall of President Dilma Rousseff's government and the rise of the agribusiness-friendly Temer government, land speculators appear emboldened, stating brazenly that they operate outside the law. Indeed, Agamenon and his fellow speculators openly revealed their plans to the local media. This is what the local newspaper, sympathetic to Agamenon, wrote at the time:

> Farmers are preparing to mobilise to defend property rights, which they see as threatened by the ineffectiveness of the federal authorities in the region. Their first action will take place in the next few days when they intend to evict those who have illegally occupied land by KM Mil (Piran, 2016).

The following day, a group of six armed men attacked the camp, firing shots in the air and shouting threats. No one was injured and the settlers believed that the gunmen intended only to intimidate them. Before the men left, they promised to return shortly and told the peasants to prepare for something much worse, ratcheting up the violence, just as Agamenon had said.

But Alenquer, highly experienced in these sorts of clashes, made an unusual move: in January 2017, he published a YouTube video in which he accused Agamenon Menezes and Neri Prazeres, the former mayor of Novo Progresso, of being land thieves and of threatening to kill him. The two denied his charges and have said they will sue him for defamation. But the attacks on the camp have stopped, for now, probably because of the publicity. In early 2018, the settlers were clinging on precariously to their plots, though they were still being threatened by gunmen. At the same time, members of the AJ Vilela group had, remarkably, gone to court, claiming that the land was theirs. It is impossible to predict the outcome in this murky world on the Amazon frontier, but prospects for the landless families were not good.

Conflicts of the kind described here are common today on the Amazon frontier, where land theft is the easiest and quickest way to make money. Probably to play down his own land grabbing activities, Agamenon told us: 'We are all land thieves here! There is no citizen who is not a land thief, because we are all illegally occupying federal land'. Cattle rancher Lincoln Queiroz Brasil would beg to differ, noting that his family did not steal its land. In the late 1970s and 80s, impoverished families, largely from southern Brazil, arrived in Novo Progresso by way of the newly opened BR-163. Many signed contracts with INCRA, the land colonisation institute, agreeing to pay for land plots in 10 annual instalments. The Queiroz were one of those families, and Lincoln told us that he remembers his scrupulously honest father travelling each year to Itaituba on the Tapajós river, at the time a difficult journey, to make the payment. But many families didn't bother paying.

Despite the exceptions, Agamenon is right to suggest that land thieving is very common. The absence of a strong law enforcement presence in the region has resulted in land thieves taking over huge tracts of public land, some covering tens of thousands of acres. In an earlier interview, Agamenon himself had bragged to one of us of being the owner of 70,000 hectares – even though it's illegal to claim such vast areas. The Brazilian Constitution sets the maximum size for a plot of public land held by a private individual at 2,500 hectares. Anything larger than that requires congressional authorisation.

Beating the constitution

Land thieves have found a way round the Brazilian Constitution: they divide the tract they want to own into subplots, each about 2,500 hectares in size. Then they get another individual – famously called a *laranja* (an orange), possibly because an orange is made up of a number of segments – to register the subplot in his or her name. Queiroz said that in Novo Progresso a land grabber can easily purchase a so-called 'citizen kit', which provides all the documents that a *laranja* requires – an identity card, electoral registration, and so on. The kits are very cheap: 'If you're a friend of the supplier, you might even be given it for nothing', laughed Queiroz. The land thief then finds an 'owner', who is generally a very poor person, pleased to earn a pittance for his or her participation in the scheme. This person can then put him or herself forward as the owner of the land, should IBAMA ever come round asking questions or seeking a fine for deforestation.

Over the last decade, the perpetrators of land theft have changed. In the past, cattle ranchers were likely to grab land for themselves for cattle rearing. Now the name of the game is forest clearance, dubbed 'speculative clearance' by the NGO IMAZON. Queiroz explained to us how it works: 'A person takes over a forested area of public land and fells the forest. He doesn't produce anything on this land, but merely clears it and sells it. And, just by felling the trees, he increases the value of the land 100 or 200 times'.

The buyers of this newly cleared land will usually raise cattle. These purchasers range from large landowners coming from Mato Grosso or Goiás, who are generally aware of the illegality of their purchase, to more naive small-scale farmers, who have sold everything they owned elsewhere to buy what they falsely believe to be a properly registered property in the Amazon. In the process, the land speculators make huge profits, with each tract of stolen land bringing in, on average, R$20 m (US$6.4 m), according to calculations by the independent MPF.

So it is that land theft has become divorced from farming. It is now through illegal 'speculative clearance' of public lands that the big money is to be made. Thus, deforestation becomes a business in its own right. Queiroz told us that 'the largest deforesters in the region do not own a single head of cattle'. His comment is backed up by a recently published study, showing that those clearing forest along the Novo Progresso section of the BR-163 have not planted or created anything, except spectacular profits for themselves, derived from the huge boom in the value of cleared Amazon real estate (Torres et al., 2017).

The Amazon deforestation racket has gained so much momentum, and become so lucrative, that after engaging in it for over a decade one famous land speculator, Ezequiel Castanha, brazenly began offering turnkey operations: he formed a partnership with a person who had taken over a large area of forest, providing him with everything he needed to clear the tract – 'oranges' with documentation, poor labourers to cut trees and to seed pastures, and much more. At the end, when the land was sold, Castanha took a hefty share of the profits. Eventually, Castanha was arrested in Operation Castanheira (named after him), which was carried out by the MPF, the federal police, and IBAMA.

Deforestation in the Novo Progresso region has been on the rise – as it was in the Amazon as a whole from 2014 to 2016, though it declined by 16 per cent in 2017 (Butler, 2017a; Butler, 2017b). Prospects are not good: at the end of March 2017, the Temer government slashed by over 50 per cent the budget of the Ministry of the Environment, which is responsible for the two main environment bodies – IBAMA, which implements the federal government's environment policies, and the ICMBio, which runs the federal government's conservation units. That meant that the forces protecting the Amazon have become even smaller and more understaffed. For the rainforest and the landless peasants, this was very bad news but, as the government well knew, the land thieves were delighted.

After our interview with Agamenon da Silva Menezes, we headed north to Santarém and ended our trip. But Maurício returned in 2017 for a couple more forays into the forest in the Tapajós river basin. The first was taken, after a tip-off, to see illegal logging in action. During that trip he learned just how closely the *Bancada Ruralista* – and thus the federal government – responds to demands from the *Bancada*'s backers in the Amazon.

The trade unionist Aluisio Sampaio, known as Alenquer, who accompanied us to the KM Mil settlement (see pp 134–138), was assassinated at home, with eight shots in the head, on 11 October 2018.

References

All web references were checked and still available in June/July 2018 unless otherwise stated.

Butler, R.A. (2017a) 'Deforestation drops 16% in the Brazilian Amazon', *Mongabay* [article] <https://news.mongabay.com/2017/10/deforestation-drops-16-in-the-brazilian-amazon/>

Butler, R.A. (2017b) 'Brazil: deforestation in the Amazon increased 29% over last year', *Mongabay* [article] <https://news.mongabay.com/2016/11/brazil-deforestation-in-the-amazon-increased-29-over-last-year/>

Piran, A. (2016) 'Produtores se organizam contra investida de invasores ligados ao MST em Novo Progresso', *Folha do Progresso* [website] <http://www.folhadoprogresso.com.br/produtores-se-organizam-contra-investida-de-invasores-ligados-ao-mst-em-novo-progresso/>

Torres, M., Doblas, J. and Alarcon, D.F. (2017) *'Dono é quem desmata: conexões entre grilagem e desmatamento no sudoeste paraense'*, São Paulo: Urutu-branco; Altamira: Instituto Agronômico da Amazônia <https://www.socioambiental.org/pt-br/noticias-socioambientais/dono-e-quem-desmata>

CHAPTER 14
Warming wood and wildcat mining

Unknown to people outside the region, many of the fortune hunters beside the BR-163 highway have switched from illegal logging to the illegal mining of cassiterite, the mineral from which tin is made. But, while loggers can extract timber under the cover of the forest canopy, mining activities are much more visible. So, in a clear demonstration of the close link between the rural lobby in congress and land grabbers in Pará, Brazil's lawmakers are pushing through changes in the law to legitimise the miners' occupation of the forest.

The Amazon is the sort of wild place where you often go looking for one thing but find another. So it was when we travelled in May 2017 to observe illegal logging operations within federal conservation units beside the BR-163, linking Santarém with Cuiabá.

What we expected to find was a serious crime involving illegal timber extraction on federal lands and possible infringement of labour laws, with workers held in conditions analogous to slavery. What we encountered instead was a broader range of criminal activities that helped to explain legislation that had just been rushed through Brazil's National Congress and was awaiting President Temer's signature to turn over very large swathes of protected Amazon to those seeking to exploit them.

Using satellite images, experts had identified illegal logging activities to the east of the BR-163, just south of the town of Vila de Três Bueiros, in the rural district of Trairão, in Pará. To reach the illegal logging camp, we needed to drive along a precarious dirt road that crossed the Branco river on a bridge built by the loggers themselves. After a few miles, our truck got stuck and we got out to push. As we sank deeper into the mud, a man aged about 40 appeared from the direction of the river. Visibly exhausted and initially mistrustful, he said he'd come from a *garimpo*, an illicit mine. That was the first inkling we had that, in addition to illegal loggers, there were wildcat miners operating inside the conservation unit illegally extracting cassiterite, the ore from which tin is refined.

The miner, on the verge of collapse, grudgingly told us he'd left the mine due to the terrible working conditions and because he hadn't

Photo 14.1 Illegal sawmill beside the BR-163 in the region of Trairão.
Photo by Daniel Paranaiba

been paid. He'd been walking since the previous day, initially with a companion, who had given up, completely worn out. Taking one last look eastward from where he'd come, he walked quickly west. Then a logger arrived on a tractor and, thanks to his vast experience of Amazonian mud, we were soon hauled out. He warned us in a friendly, unembarrassed way: 'The bridge you need to cross doesn't exist anymore. We destroyed it so IBAMA and ICMBio won't disturb us. Without a bridge, they can only get there by helicopter'.

We weren't sure whether to believe the logger, but, just to be sure, we detoured south to where the BR-163 crosses the Branco. There we rented a canoe with an outboard motor and travelled upriver for an hour to where the bridge should have been. Sure enough, when we rounded a bend in the river, we saw that the bridge had been wrecked, while a dilapidated ferryboat was moored on the east bank at the border of the conservation unit. So the logger had been truthful: the illegal loggers decided who came across and who didn't.

Another surprise at the ferry port: six men were stranded on the west bank, trying to get hold of the cables to haul the ferry over. Reluctant to say much, they confirmed that they weren't working

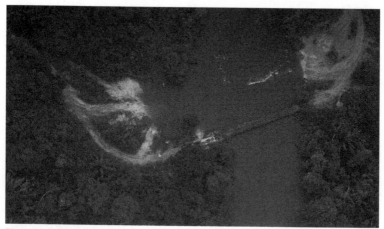

Photo 14.2 Bridge damaged by illegal loggers over the Branco River.
Photo by Daniel Paranayba

for loggers. They, too, were miners who had fallen out with the mine owner, who, they said, had 'done them over'. Trying to get away, they had set up a temporary camp two days earlier and now had little food and no drinking water. The predicament in which these men found themselves was no surprise: impoverished workers at clandestine mines are almost always severely exploited by the mine owners, who make fortunes at their expense. Something similar goes on with illegal logging operations in the Amazon, where sawmill owners, hiding behind a façade of legality, exploit local rural labourers, who often work in slave-like conditions (Lazzeri, 2017).

In our search for illegal loggers on federal lands, we hadn't expected to find, instead, illegal miners. But, as we learned first-hand, for the wealthy men behind such operations, it makes no difference whether they are extracting timber or tin: what is important is to make money.

False licences and slave labour

Indeed, both the logging and the mining were, ironically, a response to government efforts to control deforestation. In February 2006, the federal government created a corridor of conservation units on both sides of the BR-163 (see Chapter 8 and the 'Sustainable BR-163 Plan', Chapter 11) in an attempt to end illegal deforestation, which had grown exponentially due to the access the road offered.

The conservation units had not been implemented, but the very act of creating them had stopped most deforestation, since it was mainly land thieves who were clearing the forest at that time with the intention of selling the deforested land at high prices to cattle ranchers (see Chapter 13). Once the conservation units were created, it meant the land could not be as easily bought or sold for big profits, so the cutting declined.

But other ways of exploiting the land and making money were found. According to Juan Doblas, from the Geoprocessing Laboratory of the ISA, 'while deforestation [for cattle ranching] ended, the plundering of the forest by loggers gained momentum'. This activity was more difficult to monitor and control because the loggers do not clear the entire forest, but extract only the valuable trees. The severe damage they do to the understorey, officially called 'forest degradation', mostly goes undetected by satellite monitoring, which records only what is known as 'forest devastation'– the clear-cutting of rainforest.

According to studies, almost all timber leaving this region leaves illegally, as it is mainly harvested on indigenous lands and conservation units. But, once cut, the wood is transported, traded, and even exported as if it had been logged legally. Public Prosecutor Fabiana Schneider explained that there are various ways of 'warming' wood, as the scheme for legalising illegal timber is called. 'The techniques go from attaching licences granted for one area [where logging is permitted] to timber plundered from protected areas, to using sophisticated devices, such as licence cloning, or even to the hacking of the computers of federal environmental bodies to print licences'.

The claims on these licences to the origin of the timber are often patently false. We were shown a licence issued in 2007 for timber in a sawmill yard owned by Valmir Climaco, now mayor of the town of Itaituba. According to this document, the timber was bought in the city of Belém, close to the Atlantic Ocean, and had been transported 1,132 kilometres (703 miles) inland, up the Amazon to Itaituba on the Tapajós river. Such a provenance is preposterous, and all the more suspicious given the presence of timber-rich conservation units located near the sawmill. Clearly, law enforcement is either grossly negligent or, as seems more likely, corrupt in monitoring such licences.

We tracked Climaco down at the Itaituba town garage, packed full of broken-down public vehicles. After we showed him the licence he replied, with no signs of embarrassment: 'We get timber from many different places. It must be wood that we bought in Belém, unprocessed, to cut into planks in our mill'. Not a convincing explanation, as, according to the licence, the wood had already been processed when it was purchased. As for the absurd cost of transporting timber so far? The mayor, who has been fined millions of dollars for environmental crimes, had a ready, if patronising, answer: 'My dear, do you know what is the cheapest means of transport in the world? It's by river'.

Luiz Carlos Tremonte, president of the Union of Timber Industries of Southwest Pará (SIMASPA, Sindicato das Indústrias Madeireiras do Sudoeste do Pará) for many years, was much blunter: 'You get approval for a forestry management project in one area, which has little wood, and extract the timber from an area beside it or from anywhere else. The licence you get from the project "warms" the timber. Is it illegal to do this? Yes, but it's what happens and everyone knows about it'. Tremonte is an avid supporter of the timber industry. He argues that logging is so healthy for the forest that the government ought to create a programme to pay loggers for taking out timber because 'the logger extends the life of the forest'. Even so, he openly admits, 'the timber industry operates illegally'.

In the Amazon, it is quite common for those committing environmental crimes, such as Tremonte and Climaco, to hold political office in local government. Another example: the mayor of Trairão, Valdinei José Ferreira, nicknamed Django, also a logger, has been fined millions of dollars for illegal logging, though his profits probably far exceed the total of fines. He and his fellow loggers regard environmental crime and the fines it may bring as a bureaucratic detail – simply a cost of doing business. When we asked Climaco if the loggers face problems in their logging operations, he replied on camera: 'It's easy today to extract timber. What is difficult is to sell it without documentation'.

Fabiana Schneider explained that illegal logging is 'highly profitable and socially acceptable, or even seen [in the region] as something good, so the criminals are falsely seen as successful businessmen and creators of jobs'. According to the prosecutor, this aura of public approval covers up the fact that 'crimes are being committed – contemporary slavery, rural homicide, invasion of public lands, stealing and receiving public property, along with a huge chain of corruption'.

Far from being viewed as a minor offence, 'this kind of crime needs to be seen for what it is: criminal organisations plundering one of our greatest environmental riches – the forest and its biodiversity', Schneider said.

For Tremonte, a major problem that forces the timber sector to operate illegally stems from the country's labour legislation, which, according to him, 'is implemented very strictly in the region. You [the boss] are always wrong'. The boss, he says, 'is seen by the state as the enemy, and the boss is not the enemy, quite the contrary'.

His opinion isn't shared by Friar Xavier Plassat, co-ordinator of the Campaign Against Slave Labour run by the Catholic Church's Pastoral Land Commission (CPT). A Dominican friar internationally known for his struggle to combat contemporary slavery, Plassat says that it is not just a question of the loggers not complying with the country's labour laws. He told us: 'The research on this issue shows that it is impossible to have illegal logging without slave labour. The reason is simple: logging in this region is born illegal, criminal, because it is based on the use of fraudulent licences, which is the only way loggers can extract timber in areas where logging is banned. So this criminal activity can only be carried out if it is invisible. This means that it must use slave labour, zero infrastructure, zero trail, the ability to appear and then disappear back into the forest'.

We interviewed a worker who had been involved in illegal logging in the Uruará region, along the Pará section of the Transamazon Highway. For understandable reasons, he didn't give his name: 'We live in an awful way. It's perhaps best when they don't send food, for then we have to hunt. If not, we're given rotten meat and food that's gone off', he explained. 'We only have water from the *igarapés* (creeks) to drink and, if there isn't a creek nearby, tractors bring us 200-litre drums and the water stays there until it turns green. But it's a choice between drinking that or going thirsty. So we drink'.

These life-threatening conditions are found not only in the forest camps. A teacher from a community near Trairão, who also didn't want to be named, told us that among the 13- to 15-year-old children in her school, several had fingers and hands permanently injured from accidents while helping with illegal logging, something on which the village's livelihood depends. But slave labour is not confined to illegal logging. It is also found in the mines.

Cassiterite fever

On our trip, we learned that the focus of environmental crime in the region we were exploring has changed, with mining now gaining prominence over logging. 'You're out of touch with what's going on here', said one miner, who works illegally inside Jamanxim National Park. 'The road arrived here because of logging, but now the big money is in mining'. And it's no longer gold mining as in the past. The new fever is for cassiterite.

We decided to see what was happening in the forest. Unable to reach our destination by road or river, we decided to go by air. We took off from Itaituba in a single-engined plane. It was a tense flight, under heavy rain, with one door open so we could film and take photos. What we found after an hour's flight took our breath away: creeks and the surrounding vegetation destroyed, mine machinery operating freely, and many holes in the ground – mining probably done by slave labour, just as the labourer we met on the road had told us.

After our trip, in the second week of June 2017, IBAMA undertook an operation to dismantle the criminal groups mining for cassiterite and gold in the region's conservation units. According to Renê Luiz de Oliveira, IBAMA's co-ordinator for environmental monitoring, 'illicit acts were happening everywhere we looked'. And that damage to the Amazon rainforest and its rivers could get very much worse, thanks to a bill currently going through congress.

On our trip, it struck us forcefully just how closely President Temer and the congress align their legislative actions to the agenda of the *Bancada Ruralista*, the rural lobby that dominates Brazilian politics, and how the *Bancada* itself caters to the immediate demands for profit made by their wealthy backers in the countryside – with little regard for the impact on the nation's environmental and social future.

'Today, I don't want the land to log, but to mine', one land thief told us, claiming to own several thousand hectares within the national park of Jamanxim. He had already plundered the area for valuable timber, 'warming' his logs with false certificates. However, mining is far more visible from the air than logging, which is a problem for him and others like him, when the area they want to mine is also part of a conservation unit. This helped to explain the new provisional measures (MP 756 and MP 758) that President Temer was initiating at the time. Among other alterations, the aim of the MPs was to drastically reduce the size of Jamanxim National Park, while also downgrading the protection of a large part of the national forest of Jamanxim, converting this land to an APA, where both logging and mining are allowed (see Chapter 11).

In essence, Temer and the congress were attempting, with the stroke of a pen, to legalise and legitimise illegal Amazon logging and mining and to turn over vast swathes of federally protected rainforest to wealthy land thieves. After we returned from our trip, Temer was forced to veto the measures in the face of strong protests at home and abroad. But the government hasn't given up: the environment ministry took a bill to congress which reintroduced most of the changes planned for the Jamanxim National Park. In early 2018, the bill was still making its way through congress.

Still, the *Bancada Ruralista* isn't getting its way on all fronts. Apart from the opposition from activists, environmentalists, and NGOs, which has sometimes forced the government to withdraw bills from congress, indigenous and riverine communities are also organising and resisting on the ground. This has led to remarkable alliances, as we discovered on our final trip.

Reference

Lazzeri, T. (2017) 'Investigation reveals slave labor conditions in Brazil's timber industry', *Mongabay* [article] <https://news.mongabay. com/2017/03/investigation-reveals-slave-labor-conditions-in-brazils-timber-industry/> [Last accessed July 2018]

CHAPTER 15

Old enemies work together*

In the light of the failure of the authorities to demarcate the boundaries of their collectively owned land, the inhabitants of the small community of Montanha–Mangabal, beside the Tapajós river, are doing it themselves in a process known as 'auto-demarcation'. Unusually, they are receiving assistance from indigenous groups, whom they have long regarded as enemies. The new collaboration, which is being repeated elsewhere, springs from the growing awareness of indigenous people and riverine communities that only by working together do they have a chance of defeating their common enemies.

Solimar Ferreira dos Anjos felt a sense of connection one morning in November 2017 as he made his way along a stream in the rainforest, clambering over tree trunks, branches, and rocks. 'It's a great privilege for me', said the 49-year-old. 'I'm sure that my father, when he was young, travelled along these paths when he was tapping for rubber. He always wanted to bring me here and finally I'm doing it'.

Solimar is among a group of about 40 people marking out the boundaries of the 550-square-kilometre community of Montanha–Mangabal, which they and other residents inhabit in the state of Pará, beside the Tapajós river. The community, formed more than a century ago by European- and African-descended rubber tappers who intermarried with members of local indigenous groups, won the right in 2013 to become an Agro-Extractive Settlement after a protracted political and bureaucratic struggle. That status gives community members exclusive rights to the land and to its forest products, provided they collect this produce – Brazil nuts and hearts of palm, for instance – in an environmentally sound manner and do not sell any of the land.

By law, such designations must be followed by a formal demarcation of the land by INCRA. This did not happen, prompting Montanha–Mangabal to call on the agency repeatedly to act. Meanwhile, outsiders were entering the community's territory without permission to engage in unlawful logging, gold mining, and other destructive activity. In August, Ageu Pereira, president of the umbrella Association of the Communities of Montanha–Mangabal, made the 600-kilometre

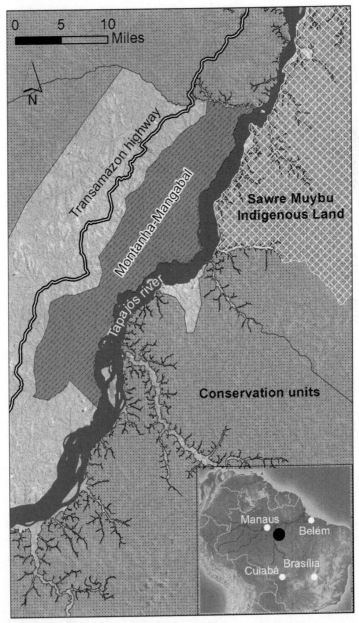

Map 15.1 The Montanha–Mangabal community.
Map by Maurício Torres

(370-mile) journey to deliver a letter to INCRA officials in Santarém in which local inhabitants demanded redress. Pereira complained in the letter and in person that he and other leaders were frequently threatened by outsiders claiming to be owners of the land, even though private ownership of Montanha–Mangabal community lands is not permitted.

The appeal had no effect, so, in early September 2017, the inhabitants took the initiative. They organised a five-day expedition to start marking out the borders of their land themselves – a process they have called *autodemarcação*, or auto-demarcation. Remarkably, they received the support of indigenous groups, who for many decades had been their sworn enemies, as the river dwellers and indigenous groups had battled over territory. A second such expedition, lasting six days, was held in November 2017 to continue the demarcation, which is now about half complete.

Juarez Saw Munduruku, the cacique, or leader, of the nearby Sawré-Muybu indigenous community, says that his people now have common cause with non-indigenous riverbank dwellers such as those of Montanha–Mangabal. Sawré-Myubu, just across the Tapajós river from Montanha–Mangabal, is one of a number of groupings of the Munduruku Indians who inhabit the Tapajós river valley. As Saw Munduruku states, 'We are threatened in the same way by the government's projects, gold miners, and loggers, so we've made this alliance'.

Ageu Pereira and Francisco Firmino da Silva, a community leader in Montanha–Mangabal, helped the Munduruku to demarcate the indigenous territory of Sawré-Muybu in 2014. As a result of this action, the Munduruku were able in 2016 to kick-start the process of getting their land the official indigenous territory designation they had been seeking for many years. Their new status was a factor in the August 2016 decision by IBAMA to refuse a licence for a large hydroelectric dam known as São Luiz do Tapajós, at a downstream site on the river. That's because the dam's reservoir would have flooded part of the indigenous territory and thus required relocation of the Indians, which is forbidden under the Brazilian Constitution. The project remains suspended. 'Now it is our time to help, and I brought 24 warriors, men and women, with me', Saw Munduruku explained while taking part in the initial demarcation in September.

The Sateré-Mawé Indians, whose land spans the states of Pará and Amazonas, have also sent warriors to help. In September 2017,

Photo 15.1 Chico Caititu from Montanha–Mongabal.
Photo by Maurício Torres

indigenous and non-indigenous participants marked out just over 18 kilometres (11 miles) of the boundary, which measures about 70 kilometres (43 miles) in all. Along the way, they discovered that in an area just over a mile from the Transamazon Highway, palms and other trees had been felled. While the community harvests the berries from wild palms without harming the trees, the outsiders had destroyed the trees to extract heart of palm, a valuable commodity. Moreover, in a clear sign that the trespassers intended to return, members of the demarcation crew encountered five rough tracks hacked out of the forest to link the area with the Transamazon Highway.

It is this kind of activity that worries the community. During the expedition, Firmino da Silva – a highly respected leader of Montanha–Mangabal who is widely known as Chico Caititu – explains why, in addition to marking the boundaries, he and other crew members were putting up notices telling outsiders to keep out. 'We're making it clear what is their land and what is ours', he says. 'In the past people have said: "I don't know what is my land". I think that from today everyone who arrives from the road will know where our land is and understand that they can't come on to it'. But the outsiders didn't take kindly to the notices. On returning and seeing them, they began threatening Montanha–Mangabal families.

Unable to get INCRA's attention, the families turned to the MPF, an independent body of federal prosecutors (see Chapter 2). At the end of October 2017, the ministry supported the community, issuing a statement declaring auto-demarcation a legitimate right and instructing gold miners, loggers, and heart of palm foragers to stop all activity within the settlement. Federal police displayed the notice in bars, hotels, and stores along the Transamazon highway.

Pressured by the MPF and press reports, Mário Sérgio da Silva Costa, superintendent of INCRA's Santarém office, visited the community on 17 November 2017 in the company of four other INCRA officials, meeting with inhabitants and Paulo de Tarso Oliveira, a prosecutor with the MPF. Says Oliveira: 'The Brazilian state is weakened, finances are very bad, the political orientation from the government isn't geared to social rights, but even so it is important to believe in the institutions and to demand that they carry out their constitutional and institutional role'. Costa encouraged families to keep up the pressure: 'It's important that you denounce what is going on … that the MPF snaps at our heels'.

INCRA agreed to take over the demarcation, making its own measurements and posting its own notices, but it sent only three employees to establish the 71-kilometre (43-mile) boundary through the hilly and thickly forested terrain. Community leaders concluded that, with such a small crew, INCRA would take months, and outsiders would have too much time to continue their incursions, so they decided to carry out the second auto-demarcation.

The 18 kilometres (11 miles) they marked out during the expedition that took place from 22 to 28 November 2017 brought the demarcation total to 36 kilometres (22 miles), with 35 kilometres (21 miles) now remaining. Among the indigenous groups taking part were the Munduruku and five other groups from the Trombetas river valley. This time they unexpectedly encountered a group of gold miners. Most of the miners stopped work once demarcation crew members showed them the notices they were nailing to trees. But one miner became angry, saying: 'So we'll see who is powerful down here! … All this land belongs to Jesus. He is the only true owner! And now you come and say it's yours!'

Though the tension brought on by such incidents remains, Montanha–Mangabal residents are feeling more optimistic. An elderly inhabitant, Dona Maria de Nazaré Oliveira, says that residents are regaining the determination they showed 15 years ago, when they

Photo 15.2 Nelison Saw Munduruku, a young Munduruku Indian, consulting his GPS. Photo by Fernanda Moreira

mobilised the community and went to court to prevent a real estate company from taking over their territory by using forged land titles. 'We were very united then', Dona Nazaré says. With many more outsiders moving into the region, she adds, the community once again must take action: 'Today it's very good that we are marking out our land, because it will give us security'. Solimar Ferreira dos Anjos agrees: 'It's already a victory to be here today and I'm sure we're going to be more united than ever in the future'.

During the September demarcation expedition, old and young worked side by side. A 17-year-old Munduruku Indian, Nelison Saw Munduruku, used his GPS device to mark out the boundaries while Chico Caititu, aged 68, drew on knowledge he had acquired through his many years of roaming the forest. 'My GPS is in my head', he said. So is his knowledge of tricks for rainforest travel, such as using creepers as a rough compass. Says Caititu: 'Creepers climb around trees only from the side of the rising sun to the setting sun'.

As the demarcation crews advanced through the forest, younger members hunted wild animals to provide them with food. On the first expedition, the oldest indigenous warrior, cacique Chico Índio, helped

Munduruku women each night to build a rustic stove made of wood and straw. Using water from nearby streams, they cooked a stew of meat from peccaries, caimans, the razor-billed curassow (Pauxi tuberosa) bird, and other game caught by young people on the expedition. At night, the Montanha–Mangabal inhabitants and the Indians recalled the early days when they could wander at will in the forest. Though the two groups, at different historical moments, have rejected the territorial restraints imposed on them, they share memories of the inroads being made into their region and agree that marking their boundaries is now the best means of protecting their lands.

This new collaboration between indigenous and non-indigenous communities may spawn further such initiatives. One might involve the Sateré-Mawé people of the Andirá-Marau Indigenous Territory, which is located on the border of Pará and Amazonas states, between the Tapajós and Madeira rivers. The Sateré-Mawé say that much of their traditional land lies outside the territory officially allocated to them and want the reserve expanded. Bernardino Mikilis dos Santos, their elderly cacique, made a 10-hour boat trip with another member of his community in September to join those taking part in the initial demarcation work. 'The union here between the Sateré, our Munduruku relatives, and riverine communities gives us strength', he said. 'I suffered during the long trip but I'm very happy to be with you. It is the first time that the Sateré took part in a auto-demarcation. And now I want to do the same thing on our land'.

All participants seemed excited by their alliance. 'I don't know how to thank enough the Munduruku and the other Indians', said Ezequiel Lobo, a Montanha–Mangabal community leader in charge of organising the future expeditions needed to complete the demarcation. 'We're going to demarcate and we're going to struggle. We're going to be with the Indians until the end'. Soon people from Montanha–Mangabal will be helping the Munduruku once again, this time to clear the rough paths cut during the auto-demarcation of the Sawré-Muybu Indigenous Territory.

Few doubt that difficult days lie ahead, with all the pressure to open up new road, rail, and river transport corridors through the Tapajós river basin for agricultural exports, particularly soya (see Chapter 8). This rapid opening up of the Amazon, while cheered by business interests, has drawn criticism from scientists and others concerned that the development projects will cause future rounds of forest clearing, thereby accelerating habitat loss and climate change.

The need for corrective action is beginning to take hold in the business world, including the livestock industry, which is estimated to account for 15 per cent of all greenhouse gas output. A new analysis from Farm Animal Investment Risk and Return (FAIRR), an investor initiative that is boosting awareness of the risks of factory farming, says that a tax on meat is inevitable within 5–10 years, as the world struggles to curb the greenhouse gas emissions that spur climate change.

Such action might eventually quench demand for Brazilian soya and beef, but it is unclear whether this would occur soon enough for communities in the Tapajós valley. Meanwhile, those communities vow to mark off and defend their boundaries as best they can. Cacique Juarez Saw Munduruku, for one, is determined to collaborate to that end with indigenous and non-indigenous neighbours alike: 'That's what my life is about now: helping these people mark out their land, because this will help them and future generations'.

Note

* Fernanda Moreira contributed to this article, which was first published in the December 2017 edition of *EcoAméricas*, a monthly report on Latin American environmental issues and trends.

Conclusion

Travelling in the Tapajós river valley involves moving between different historical times, from a region that has been conquered to one that is still in dispute. The state is not absent in the region but actively interfering to promote the interests of the land grabbers and agribusiness. Leading environmental agencies are promoting strategies for combating forest felling that are at best ineffectual and are being hijacked by agribusiness and big corporations to be used as dangerous 'greenwash'. Even so, resistance among the traditional and indigenous communities, the real guardians of the forest, has made advances and achieved significant victories.

The sociologist José de Souza Martins, who carried out extensive research in the Amazon in the late 20th century and has thought deeply about the region, once said that the bullet that leaves the gunman's weapon, as he carries out the orders of a land grabber, not only spans the space between the two of them but also crosses the historical distance that separates two worlds (Martins, 1996). This sensation of moving from one world to another was a constant in our journey.

In the early part of our trip, when we were travelling through the Cerrado and visiting newly founded towns, such as Sorriso and Sinop, we had the impression that we were moving through a region devastated by an invading army applying a scorched earth policy. In place of the forest and the traditional and indigenous communities, which had interacted harmoniously with the forest and the rivers, the conquerors had imposed a new order, where land, cleared of forest, was concentrated in the hands of a few big farmers, and agribusiness, with its high consumption of pesticides and close links with foreign grain corporations, called the shots. We not only saw this modern Brazil, with its wealthy elite enriched by the soya boom, but we also discovered, behind the glitter, a few remaining peasant settlements, squeezed by land concentration and land grabbing on to small parcels of land.

As we travelled north, however, moving from the Cerrado into tropical forest, we entered an earlier historical period. Vast tracts of forest were still standing, and traditional and indigenous communities were fighting to protect their land. Indeed, resistance against the invasion was so strong that the advance troops of the new order were assassinating a large number of rural leaders to quell the opposition. The lawlessness was reminiscent of the political climate encountered by Souza Martins and one of the authors in the now 'tamed' region in the Cerrado in the north of the state of Mato Grosso during the last years of the military dictatorship in the late 1970s and early 1980s.

But the two worlds are not always divided geographically. Very often, the most modern and the most archaic coexist in the same space, as pointed out decades ago by Martins (Martins, 1997). An example is found in one of the large hydroelectric dams built on the Teles Pires river. During the developmental fever that took hold of Brazil in the early years of the 21st century, when the economy was growing fast, mega hydroelectric dams were built on most of the main Amazon tributaries. At the Teles Pires dam, we saw the strange fusion between, on the one hand, the company's pride in using the latest hydroelectric technology and the most sophisticated construction techniques and, on the other, the company's bloodthirsty zeal, typical of the *bandeirantes* (16th-century Portuguese buccaneers), to ride roughshod over indigenous people and traditional communities, desecrating their way of life and their cosmology. With no compunction, they dynamited the Munduruku's most sacred site, callously destroying the resting place of the spirits of the Indians' ancestors, where their spirits, too, will go after death. In that single explosion, they shattered the Indians, in life and in death.

The dominant discourse in political analysis stresses the 'absence of the state' in rural areas in the Amazon but this is not exactly what we encountered. We found that land grabbers and other members of the rural elite had very close relations with the most powerful group in congress – the *Bancada Ruralista* (rural lobby) – and that the state was constantly devising ways of providing juridical and political backing for their attempts to reverse the gains made by traditional communities and indigenous people in the 1988 constitution. Often the state expresses the same racism and willingness to reproduce the savagery of the 16th-century Conquest of the Americas as the companies. At times, this is expressed literally: we discovered that, beside the same Teles Pires river, the federal police had co-ordinated a highly inept operation to combat illegal artisanal gold mines which, because of the police's failure to understand indigenous norms and conventions, had ended tragically, with one Indian being assassinated, others seriously wounded, and a whole village traumatised.

But at other times the invading forces uses more subtle tactics. A shocking example of the effectiveness of this approach came early in our trip in the town of Juara, where a large statue in the town's main square commemorates the arrival in the 1970s of the first settlers from the south of Brazil. A Munduruku Indian, who belongs to a people who have inhabited the region for at least 10,000 years, pointed to the statue and told us that it marked the arrival of the first 'people' into the region. He was expressing two inter-linked prejudices imposed from outside: that there were no 'people' in the region before the arrival of the colonisers; and those living there before had not reached the condition of 'human beings'. It is a distressing indication of the power of an alien, dominant ideology, when an indigenous people starts dating the region's history from the arrival 40 years ago of those who decimated them.

Exacerbating climate change

If the rise in global warming is to be held below 2°C , as agreed at the UN climate talks in Paris in 2015, it is imperative that effective action is taken to end deforestation in the Amazon. It is true that the rate at which the forest is being felled has fallen. In 1994–5, it reached the frighteningly high level of 28,000 square kilometres – an area larger than Wales (20,743 square kilometres). Widespread international protests ensued, and the level of devastation has been falling since, even though there was another peak in 2003–4. In 2016–17, 6,624 square kilometres, an area the size of Lincolnshire, were felled; even this smaller territory covers four times the area of Greater London.

At a time when, at last, the world is beginning to talk seriously about reducing greenhouse gas emissions, it makes no sense to continue cutting down the Amazon forest, as this deals a double blow to the goal set in Paris. First of all, the felled trees contribute to greenhouse gases by releasing either carbon dioxide when they are burnt, as generally happens, or methane, a much more deadly greenhouse gas, when the timber rots in reservoirs (Graham-Rowe, 2005). During the latter part of the 20th century, one quarter or more of all the greenhouse gases released from all human activities, including the burning of fossil fuels, came from forest destruction across the tropical belt, from the Americas across to Africa and on to South East Asia (Bunyard, 2015). In the Amazon, the felled forest is generally replaced by pasture, which is inhabited by termites and cattle, both of which emit greenhouse gases.

The second, far more serious, reason we should be concerned by the current rate of devastation relates to the important role played by the Amazon forest in the global climate. As the trade winds from Africa blow across the Amazon basin, they carry rain-laden clouds. In a process called evapotranspiration, this rain falls on to the forest, is evaporated, rises, and once again forms clouds. The whole process is repeated five or six times as the clouds move west across the basin. When the clouds reach the Andes, they are diverted south, forming what have been called flying rivers and carrying precious rainfall to the south of Brazil and neighbouring countries (Rocha, 2014).

But, for this process to work, the forest must be of a certain size. If the felling goes on, scientists believe a tipping point will be reached, at which a large part of the forest will turn into a biologically impoverished savannah. If this happens, the trade winds will be disrupted, no longer carrying the all-important rain to the south. Just as serious, the Amazon forest will no longer act as an important carbon sink, absorbing far more carbon dioxide than it emits. Instead, it will start releasing the carbon it contains in its biomass, estimated at 120 billion tons of carbon, equivalent to 12 years of global emissions. It is difficult to imagine how we could possibly bring global warming under control if this were to happen.

When this tipping point will be reached has been a matter of scientific debate. While one earlier scientific model indicated that this point would be reached when 40 per cent of the forest is felled, a new study suggests that it will happen much sooner. It argues that 'the effects of deforestation compound the impact of fire, forest degradation, and climate change, leading to an acceleration of the expected scenario', and these factors are not built into the models. It concludes that the 'tipping point for the Amazon system to flip to non-forest ecosystems in eastern, southern, and central Amazonia [is] at 20–25% deforestation' (Lovejoy and Nobre, 2018).Conservative estimates suggest that about 18 per cent of the forest is already felled, though the considerable damage done to the forest's understorey by loggers and the harm caused by forest fires are not reflected in this figure (Butler, 2017). As a result, the scientist Antônio Donato Nobre (who is, as it happens, Carlos Nobre's brother) believes that the 'crossing of the point of no return … is uncomfortably close' (Nobre, 2014).

Indeed, he believes that the severe droughts and fires that have afflicted the Amazon basin in recent years are the 'first flickerings' of what is to come.

Given the uncertainty and the seriousness of what is at stake, Antônio Donato Nobre, who has become something of an environmental activist in recent years, is calling for radical action:

> It is necessary to stop the bleeding and destruction of the forest, i.e., to halt deforestation, forest degradation and fire immediately, using any and all possible and ethical means. At the same time, bearing in mind that accumulated deforestation and degradation are the most serious factors contributing to regional climate change, developing a large-scale, effective effort to replant and restore the areas denuded of their forest cover becomes an urgent necessity (Nobre, 2014).

It is against this background that the importance of what is happening in the Tapajós valley gains weight. It is located in the heart of the Amazon basin. If it is ravaged, it will be difficult to stem the devastation spreading into the Trombetas and the Madeira river basins.

Combating the destruction

While all environmental agencies agree, in theory, with Antônio Donato Nobre on the pressing need to stop the destruction of the Amazon forest, we discovered on our trip to the Tapajós valley that some of the most powerful voices, including both The Nature Conservancy (TNC) and Greenpeace, are betting on doubtful strategies. These agencies, widely known for separating environmental factors from the broader political and social framework in their analyses, believe that pacts with corporations can be effective as an instrument of environmental control. Immersed in what has become known as ecological modernisation, based on the idea that technology will make corporate interests compatible with environmental conservation, these environmentalists have put a lot of energy into negotiating pacts that became known as the Amazon Soy Moratorium (ASM) and the Beef Agreement (Mongabay, 2009).

As we showed, these agreements were far more effective as advertising material for the agents of devastation than as a form of environmental control (see Chapter 9). In fact, by guaranteeing that soya and beef supplied by signatories to the agreements are 'sustainably produced', they end up feeding the voracity they claim to contain. Moreover, they are often cited as examples of good practice. Activists in Ghana, attempting to stop the felling of forest to pave the way for cacao plantations, are calling for the negotiation of an accord like 'the one on soya [that] worked well in the Amazon' (Maclean, 2017), while others, seeking to force Wilmar, Asia's leading agribusiness group and the largest palm oil processor and trader in the world – controlling 45 per cent of global oil trade – to behave more responsibly, say that 'the landmark soy moratorium to prevent deforestation [in the Amazon] offers a valuable lesson for palm oil industry' (Van Tran, 2016).

Another inherent incoherence in these pacts is that they relegate to the sidelines the main protagonists in the struggle to conserve the Amazon: the indigenous and tribal peoples, as they are described in the International Labour Organisation's Convention 169. It is not by chance that the best protected areas in the Amazon are indigenous lands, which have lost less of their forests than even the conservation units. The territories occupied by traditional populations are also known to be rich in biodiversity, with healthy and notably well-managed forests. So, by peddling the myth that the rapid expansion of agribusiness is compatible with the preservation of the forests, provided that it is managed by voluntary agreements, these deals divert attention away from the urgent need to bring law and order to the region, to contain agribusiness to the areas it has already devastated, and to support the real guardians of the forest. However unpopular the message may be, the world needs to bite the bullet and accept that conserving the forest will eventually lead to higher market prices for beef and soya.

These pacts are not the only kind of greenwash found in the Amazon. At a time when people all over the world are wishing to support ways of curbing deforestation, and consumers are seeking to track the forest products they consume to ensure that they are produced sustainably, destructive activities are decked out in green ribbons to create an aura of sustainability. The most monstrous example we encountered on this trip was the awarding of the Chico Mendes Award for Responsible Social and Environmental Management to the Teles Pires Hydroelectric Company, the company that had dynamited the Munduruku's most sacred site. The company also, remarkably, qualified for Kyoto Protocol carbon credits under the UN's Clean Development Mechanism (CDM).

Resistance

The forest peoples are ill-equipped and small in number when compared with the might of the invaders, who are paving roads, creating massive port complexes, and building railways. But they are pulling off unexpected feats. Their greatest success to date was to get the government to shelve the large hydroelectric dam of São Luiz do Tapajós planned for downstream on the Tapajós river. The big environmental NGOs were convinced that it was unstoppable and were already beginning to talk to the government about the conditions for its construction. But this talk of fait accompli didn't convince the Munduruku Indians and the riverine communities scattered along the middle reaches of the Tapajós.

In May 2013, Indians from various groups and riverine communities jointly occupied the building site of the largest construction work in the country – the hydroelectric dam of Belo Monte on the Xingu river. Munduruku, Juruna, Kayapó, Xipaya, Kuruaya, Asurini, Parakanã, and Arara Indians stood alongside representatives of the fishing and riverine communities of the Tapajós and Xingu rivers and envoys from the land settlements along the Transamazon Highway. Until recently, these groups had seen each other as enemies, but now the scale of the big new dam planned for the Tapajós river – and the arrogant way it was being imposed on them by the authorities – brought them together. The representatives from the Tapajós river valley were also horrified to see the damage that the Belo Monte dam was doing to their 'relatives' in the Xingu (Sullivan, 2018). It pressed home to them the need to fight hard to stop this happening to them.

Remarkably, partly as a result of indigenous protests, the Brazilian authorities suspended plans to build the São Luiz do Tapajós hydroelectric plant (Sainsbury, 2016). In late December 2017, leading government authorities said that the era of mega-dams in the Amazon was over and that it was unlikely that the São Luiz do Tapajós would ever go ahead (Branford, 2017). They cited both the falling cost of renewable energy and indigenous opposition to the big dams as reasons for the change in policy. But later the two top officials making these statements were quietly replaced. Mega-dams are back on the government's agenda (Fearnside, 2018).

There is little sign that the takeover of the region by agribusiness is faltering. Chinese companies, not known for their environmental concern, are moving in. They are talking of building both an industrial waterway along the Juruena, Teles Pires, and Tapajós rivers and a 5,311-kilometre (3,300-mile) railway connecting the Atlantic and

Pacific coasts, thus reducing 'the cost of shipping grain and minerals to Asia' (Tasch, 2015). Both projects would do a great deal of damage to both the people of the region and the environment. However, the recent victories show that big infrastructure projects can be stopped and, if resistance grows, even the agribusiness juggernaut can be halted or, at least, contained within narrow confines.

What tends to get lost in the discussion – and, indeed, perhaps in our articles – is the *joie de vivre* of the Amazon's indigenous and traditional communities, their profound love of the forest, and the enjoyment they derive from it. They can talk for hours about all the spirits and animals that live in the forest. Their conversations can be incomprehensible to outsiders. Those who don't know that white egrets, spoonbills, and kingfishers, but not owls, are fish-eaters in the Amazon, that the Jacu bird and the cācā-hawk have red throats, and that the toucan has an orange bill, will be bewildered by the stories told by the Wayapí Indians, says anthropologist Alan Tornaid Campbell (Campbell, 1995). So we end this book by transferring to the Tapajós basin something that José de Souza Martins once said:

> We need to laugh the critical laugh that denounces the ridicu-
> lousness of the protagonists, the conquerors, in their vain attempt
> to wear, and to impose, the tight cultural clothing of those who

Photo 16.1 Farmers in Montanha–Mangabal enjoying a day on their plots.
Photo by Maurício Torres

give orders or think they give orders. Don't cry for us, because Latin America isn't a funeral. Latin America is a *fiesta*, even when we are burying our dead. Because in the silence of the funerals of the victims of those who oppress us there is also the internal song of our hope, the announcement and prefiguration of our collective and permanent *fiesta* (Martins, 1996).

References

All web references were checked and still available in June/July 2018 unless otherwise stated.

Branford, S. (2018) 'Brazil announces end to Amazon mega-dam building policy', *Mongabay* [article] <https://news.mongabay.com/2018/01/brazil-announces-end-to-amazon-mega-dam-building-policy/>

Bunyard, P. (2015) 'Without its rainforest the Amazon will turn desert', *The Ecologist* [online] <https://theecologist.org/2015/mar/02/without-its-rainforest-amazon-will-turn-desert>

Butler, R. (2017) 'Calculating deforestation figures for the Amazon', *Mongabay* [online] <https://rainforests.mongabay.com/amazon/deforestation_calculations.html>

Campbell, A.T. (1995) *Getting to know Waiwai – an Amazonian ethnography*, Routledge, Oxford.

Fearnside, P. (2018) 'Damming the Amazon unfettered after Brazilian purge' <https://news.mongabay.com/2018/05/damming-the-amazon-unfettered-after-brazilian-purge-commentary/>

Graham-Rowe, D. (2005) 'Hydroelectric power's dirty secret revealed' *New Scientist* [website] <https://www.newscientist.com/article/dn7046-hydroelectric-powers-dirty-secret-revealed/>

Lovejoy, T.E. and Nobre, C. (2018) 'Amazon Tipping Point', *Science Advances*, [online] <http://advances.sciencemag.org/content/4/2/eaat2340> (published 21 February 2018)

Maclean, R. (2017) 'Chocolate industry drives rainforest disaster in Ivory Coast', *Guardian* [website] <https://www.theguardian.com/environment/2017/sep/13/chocolate-industry-drives-rainforest-disaster-in-ivory-coast>

Martins, J. (1996) 'O tempo da fronteira. Retorno à controvérsia sobre o tempo histórico da frente de expansão e da frente pioneira', *Tempo Social*, 8(1): 25–70.

Martins, J. (1997) *Fronteira: a degradação do Outro nos confins do humano*, Hucitec, São Paulo.

Mongabay (2009) 'Brazilian beef giants agree to moratorium on Amazon deforestation', *Mongabay* [online] <https://news.mongabay.

com/2009/10/brazilian-beef-giants-agree-to-moratorium-on-amazon-deforestation>

Nobre, A.D. (2014) 'The Future Climate of Amazonia: Scientific Assessment Report', *INPE-INPA* <https://www.scribd.com/document/329136378/The-Future-Climate-of-Amazonia-Report>

Nobre, C.A., Sampaio, G., Borma, L.S., Castilla-Rubio, J.C., Silva, J.S. and Cardoso, M. (2016) 'Land-use and climate change risks in the Amazon and the need of a novel sustainable development paradigm', *Proceedings of the National Academy of Sciences of the United States of America*, 113(39): 10759–68 <http://www.pnas.org/content/113/39/10759>

Rocha, J. (2014) 'Drought bites as Amazon's "flying rivers" dry up', *Climate News Network* [online] <https://climatenewsnetwork.net/drought-bites-as-amazons-flying-rivers-dry-up/>

Sainsbury, C. (2016) 'Mega-dam suspended, providing hope for indigenous people and biodiversity', *Mongabay* [website] <https://news.mongabay.com/2016/04/amazon-mega-dam-suspended-hope-indigenous-people-biodiversity/>

Salisbury, C. (2017) 'From carbon sink to source: Brazil puts Amazon, Paris goals at risk', *Mongabay* [website] <https://news.mongabay.com/2017/11/from-carbon-sink-to-source-brazil-puts-amazon-paris-goals-at-risk/>

Sullivan, Z. (2018) 'Brazil's dispossessed: Belo Monte dam ruinous for indigenous cultures', *Mongabay* [online] <https://news.mongabay.com/2016/12/brazils-dispossessed-belo-monte-dam-ruinous-for-indigenous-cultures/>

Tasch, B. (2015) 'China's $10 billion railway across South America is either bold or insane', *Business Insider* [website] <http://uk.businessinsider.com/china-plans-to-build-a-3300-mile-railway-across-south-america-2015-6?r=US&IR=T>

Tran, V. (2016) 'From chocolate ice cream to deforestation in Borneo', [online] <https://rctom.hbs.org/submission/from-chocolate-ice-cream-to-deforestation-in-borneo/>

Glossary

ABIOVE Associação Brasileira das Indústrias de Óleos Vegetais, Brazilian Association of the Vegetable Oil Industries: the vegetable oil manufacturers' trade association

APA Área de Proteção Ambiental, Environmental Protection Area: the most flexible kind of conservation unit in Brazil, in which third parties can take over land for any kind of productive activity

Aprosoja Associação dos Produtores de Soja e Milho, Association of Soya and Maize Producers: the soya farmers' trade association

Bancada Ruralista: the powerful agribusiness lobby in the National Congress

BNDES Banco Nacional de Desenvolvimento Econômico e Social, National Economic and Social Development Bank: a state-owned bank

CIMI Conselho Indígenista Misionário, Indigenous Missionary Council: the Catholic Church's indigenous council

CNA Confederação da Agricultura e Pecuária do Brasil, Confederation of Agriculture and Livestock: the landowners' trade association

CPI Comissão Parlamentar de Inquérito, Parliamentary Commission of Enquiry

EMBRAPA Empresa Brasileira de Pesquisa Agropecuária, Brazilian Agricultural and Livestock Research Company: a state-owned research institute

EPE Empresa de Pesquisa Energética, Energy Research Company: linked to Brazil's Energy Ministry

FDA Fundo de Desenvolvimento da Amazônia, Amazon Development Fund

FLONA Floresta Nacional, National Forest: a conservation unit that can only be inhabited by traditional communities but where mining and logging are permitted through a system of public concessions

Flona Fundação Nacional do Indio, National Indian Foundation: the government's indigenous agency, linked to the Ministry of Justice

IBAMA Instituto Brasileiro do Meio Ambiente, Brazilian Environmental Institute: the government's environmental agency, linked to the Environmental Ministry

ICMBio Instituto Chico Mendes de Conservação da Biodiversidade, Chico Mendes Institute for the Conservation of Biodiversity: an institute owned by the federal government

IMAZON Instituto do Homem e Meio Ambiente da Amazônia, The Institute for Man and the Environment in Amazonia: a Brazilian NGO

INCRA Instituto Nacional de Colonização e Reforma Agrária, the National Institute of Colonisation and Agrarian Reform: a government agency

INPA Instituto Nacional de Pesquisas Amazônicas, National Institute of Amazonian Research: a state-owned research institute

IPHAN Instituto do Patrimônio Histórico e Artistíco Nacional, National Institute of Historic and Artistic Heritage: linked to Brazil's culture ministries, responsible for the country's cultural assets

ISA Instituto Socioambiental, Social and Environmental Institute: a Brazilian NGO

MP *Medida Provisória*, Interim Measure: a decree that can be issued by the president without congressional approval

MPF Ministério Público Federal, Federal Public Ministry: an independent body of federal prosecutors

OPAN Operação Amazônia Nativa, Native Amazonia Operation: an NGO active in the Mato Grosso region of the Tapajós river valley

PAC Programa de Aceleração do Crescimento, Programme for the Acceleration of Growth: a government fund for investment in infrastructure

Quilombola: inhabitant of a quilombo, a community of Afro-Brazilians, composed mainly of descendants of slaves who fled the slave plantations which persisted in Brazil until 1888

SUDAM Superintendência do Desenvolvimento da Amazônia, Amazonia Development Superintendency: set up by the military government in 1966 to fund the development of the Amazon

Latin America Bureau (LAB)

LAB is an independent charitable organisation, based in London, which provides news, analysis, and information on Latin America, reporting consistently from the perspective of the region's poor, oppressed, or marginalised communities and social movements. LAB brings an alternative, critical awareness and understanding of Latin America to readers throughout the English-speaking world.

LAB is widely known for its books and operates a website, updated daily, in which it carries news and analysis on Latin America and reports from our partners and correspondents in the region (www.lab.org.uk).